# Mentorship

Second Edition

COLETTE TOACH

*Bringing out
the Treasure
in God's People*

**AMI BOOKSHOP**

www.ami-bookshop.com

# Mentorship 101

Second Edition

**ISBN-10:** 162664067X
**ISBN-13:** 978-1-62664-067-2

1st Printing April 2014
2nd Edition April 2016

Published by **Apostolic Movement International, LLC**
E-mail Address: admin@ami-bookshop.com
Web Address: www.ami-bookshop.com

# FOREWORD

## How to Use This Book

Because of the practical nature of this book, I will help you along with practical application and "Points to Remember".

## Points to Remember

 Points to remember found here!

The "Points to Remember" will be displayed in a table to help you identify them. Pay special attention to these points and write them down, to help commit them to memory.

A full list of "Points to Remember" is included at the end of the book, along with their corresponding pages for quick look up

This is not a book that you will read once and put down, but rather one you will read again and again, and each time the Lord will bring you someone new to work with. Each chapter will act as a building block for your ministry, enabling you to construct the vision that God has given to you.

 **Tools of the Trade**

This section is written to challenge you and to also bring home the principles you are learning. You will learn theoretical principles and along with that how to apply them practically to your ministry.

Are you mentoring someone right now? Pay special attention to this section in each chapter and apply the principles to your relationships. The greatest teacher is one that has lived what he teaches. So dive in and make this journey exciting! Apply and live what you are learning and you will never have a problem forgetting the essentials.

## Disciple vs. Intern

I use these terms interchangeably in this book. I like the term intern, because it covers both natural and spiritual mentorship. It also gives you a feeling of each relationship having a different intensity.

While the principles for mentorship are the same across the board, there are some you will work more intensely with than others. I also like that the word "intern" has the connotation of being "active." When you think of an intern, you see someone willing to learn, submit and get the job done.

The word disciple has been tarnished a lot in the Church because many see the relationship as a "see how we go" commitment, instead of a serious commitment to receive, learn, change and rise up into a particular position.

## Bonus Chapter on Templates and Triggers

I refer to a term that we teach in our ministry a lot. This term is, "Templates and Triggers." If you are not familiar with our teachings, I have provided a bonus chapter for you on the subject at the end of this book. If this term is new to you, then I suggest that you take a moment to go and read that chapter now before progressing.

# CONTENTS

FOREWORD ...................................................................3

    How to Use This Book .........................................3

    Points to Remember .............................................3

    Tools of the Trade ................................................3

CONTENTS ...................................................................6

CHAPTER 01: Guidelines to Mentorship ....................11

    How It all Began ..................................................11

    Guidelines to Mentorship ..................................14

    General Guidelines ............................................18

CHAPTER 02: Guidelines to Discipleship ...................29

    The Price ............................................................29

    Your Role as a Disciple .....................................36

    Understanding Pressure ....................................39

CHAPTER 03: Mentorship – The Bottom Line ............47

    Where to Begin ..................................................47

    God's Pattern for Correction .............................54

    Tools of the Trade ..............................................59

    Read With Expectation ......................................62

CHAPTER 04: Mentorship - What to Expect ..............69

    Mentorship 101 ..................................................70

    Mentorship Requirements .................................75

Colette Toach

CHAPTER 05: Start Here.................................................87

Step 1: Breaking Down Walls ...........................87

Step 2: Meet Their Needs....................................92

Step 3: Minister to Templates of the Past.................97

Step 4: Set the Conditions ..............................100

CHAPTER 06: Mentorship: Do's & Don'ts.................. 105

What Not to Do...................................................106

What to Do .........................................................110

Tools of the Trade..............................................121

Tools of the Trade..............................................121

CHAPTER 07: Phase 1 – The Mentorship Structure 127

Setting up the Structure ...................................128

Mentorship, a Step at a Time ...........................130

Step 1. Initiate Mentorship ..............................130

Step 2. Define the Mentorship Relationship..........132

Step 3. Share Your Expectations...................... 135

Step 4. Send Them to Teachings....................... 136

Step 5. Make Instructions Specific................... 139

The Instruction I Give My Disciples .................141

Tools of the Trade..............................................146

Tools of the Trade..............................................146

Step 6. The Examinations ................................. 147

The Differences Between a Mentor and Pastor ... 149

CHAPTER 08: Phase 2 - Parables, Problems & Projects ........................................................................... 155

   1. The Parable ................................................. 157

   2. Problems ................................................... 164

   3. Project ...................................................... 169

   Tools of the Trade ........................................ 171

   Tools of the Trade ........................................ 171

CHAPTER 09: Fivefold Ministry Mentorship ............ 173

   The Pressures of Apostolic Training ....................... 174

   The Pressures of Prophetic Training ...................... 176

   The Pressures of Teacher Training ......................... 178

   The Pressures of Pastoral Training ......................... 180

   The Pressures of Evangelistic Training ................... 182

CHAPTER 10: Phase 3: Chiseling and Correction .... 187

   Shaping and Sculpting ..................................... 187

   Training in Righteousness ................................. 189

   Using the Chisel ........................................... 193

   When to Chisel ............................................ 195

   Why Chiseling is Needed ................................. 199

CHAPTER 11: How to Chisel ................................. 203

   1. The Perfect Time – When It Comes Up ............... 203

   2. Use the Word When you Chisel ....................... 204

   3. Stand in the Anointing ................................. 206

   4. Chisel with Intent ...................................... 211

5. Identify the Root.................................................216

Tools of the Trade..............................................217

Tools of the Trade..............................................217

Correction .........................................................218

Chiseling............................................................221

Direct Orders ....................................................223

Tools of the Trade..............................................224

Tools of the Trade..............................................224

CHAPTER 12: Healing, Impartation & Breaking Ties
.............................................................................225

Gifts are Meant to be Special...............................225

How to Deal With Blockages and Bondages..........228

1. Identify the Root Problem – Personal Sin..........229

2. Make Them Take Responsibility .......................234

3. Identify the Template......................................238

4. Dealing With the Demonic Bondage .................239

Tools of the Trade..............................................244

Tools of the Trade..............................................244

CHAPTER 13: The Healing Process.......................245

Inner Healing ....................................................247

Impartation........................................................249

Apostolic Impartation .........................................252

Saying Goodbye .................................................253

When You Will See the Fruit................................254

CHAPTER 14: Breaking the Mentorship Ties ............ 257

  The Step by Step Process of Letting Go ................. 257

  Tools of the Trade................................................. 261

  Mentorship vs. Spiritual Parenting ........................ 261

  Summary............................................................... 267

BONUS CHAPTER: Templates and Triggers ............. 270

  The Race You Have Run Up Until Now ................... 272

  What to Watch Out For.......................................... 280

  Dealing With It – Step by Step ............................... 283

  Step 1: Identify It................................................. 283

  Step 2: Change it!................................................. 284

  Step 3: Kick the Devil Out!.................................... 286

'Point To Remember' Summary..................................... 289

Recommendations by the Author................................. 295

  Called to the Ministry........................................... 295

  How to Get People to Follow You............................ 295

  The Minister's Handbook ...................................... 296

  Strategies of War.................................................. 296

Contact Information ................................................... 297

About the Author ....................................................... 298

# CHAPTER 01:
# Guidelines to Mentorship

## How It all Began

The Lord had just opened the first big door for our ministry. It was the year 2000 and we were thrust from being stuck in a foreign land with only an Internet connection, to reaching the world.

It started with an international conference that launched us in ways we could never have imagined.

It was in this season that someone who had been in leadership for a number of years asked me, "How do you put your lessons together? How do you train all these people?"

At that time, we had already launched our prophetic school, and had been mentoring prophets into their calling for two years.

I was taken aback by the question. It did not occur to me that mentoring was something unique. I thought it was something everyone could do. I looked at the training mechanism that we had put together and I assumed that this was something everyone could do.

In my opinion at the time, you just sat down, got revelation and implemented what God gave you a step at a time. What I did not realize was that God had taught me how to mentor a step at a time. He had shown me natural principles to use when working with people.

Then in addition to those natural principles He imparted to me the wisdom and anointing I needed to shape the vessels He brought to me.

The following passage became the rock on which I built my training ministry.

> *1 Corinthians 3:11 For no other foundation can anyone lay than that which is laid, which is Jesus Christ.*
> *12 Now if anyone builds on this foundation with gold, silver, precious stones, wood, hay, straw,*
> *13 each one's work will become clear; for the Day will declare it, because it will be revealed by fire; and the fire will test each one's work, of what sort it is.*
> *14 If anyone's work which he has built on it endures, he will receive a reward.*
> *15 If anyone's work is burned, he will suffer loss; but he himself will be saved, yet so as through fire.*

God gave me the pattern to help His people, to build a successful house on the foundation He had set for His Church. I learned this process in two phases. I first learned the naturalistic side of mentorship.

Even though I got all of my principles from the Lord directly, I often found myself in the fire as He challenged me to learn and be more than I had been before. I had to become a different person and I often had to take on new skills that I never had before.

Oh, how I wish some of that just came by the "laying on of hands" and a quick impartation. No such joy! Nope, for the most part I had to learn things the hard way. There were times when I just had to put the grey matter between my ears into good use and learn things!

Then there were other times when I was trying so hard in the flesh to get everything right, that God would say to me, "This is not about your skills and works, but about my power! Now put aside your abilities and watch me work."

It took me quite some time to find that balance, and I am sure it has taken you as well. When should you be applying common sense in a mentorship relationship, and when should you be applying the power of the Spirit? Well, that is what I am here to show you.

There is no better way for me to show you though, than to take you through the process myself. So for the next few chapters you and I are going to have a special relationship. You will be my disciple and I will be your mentor.

What is the objective of this relationship? Well, that is simple. It is, "How to make you into the mentor that God has called you to be."

What is the point of this journey? It is to enable you to take all the precious treasures that God has given you through the years and to impart it to others. What is the use of having so much wealth in your life if you cannot pass it on?

So let me ask you, "What do you want your house to be made out of?" I am personally pretty keen on the Lord finding my house built out of gold, silver and precious stones. So come then, let me help you find that gold and silver and let me give you the blueprint to build that house effectively.

Then as it stands there, ready to be tested, may the power of the Holy Spirit come upon it and transform it into a city on a hill for everyone to see.

## Guidelines to Mentorship

In thinking of a good illustration for mentorship, I was reminded of the time we went to Switzerland for the first time. Their main language there is German. Therefore, I thought that I should get myself some books and teach myself German.

Have you ever tried to learn a new language by reading a book? How much fun is that? It is extremely hard. You try to figure out the phonetics and accents but it is difficult. Be that as it may, I still could not wait to get to Switzerland and use this language that I had learned.

When I got to Switzerland, I opened my mouth and began to speak what I learned. The people looked at me and answered me to everything I said with a, "Yes..."

You know how when you do not understand someone, you just play it safe by smiling, nodding your head and saying, "yes"? Well, that is exactly what they were doing to me!

I was so frustrated. I put in all this effort and no one understood a word that I said. Thankfully, God is gracious and He brought me a mentor that was a local to help me.

They spoke fluent English and they sat down and taught me German. We wrote songs together, we read the Word together in German and slowly I picked up the language. I learned more in that short time of being immersed in the language with having someone to help me, than in all those books that I had spent so much money on.

How many books have you bought and spent money on? I came to realize that although anointed materials are fantastic, it is one thing to read a book and another thing to live a book.

## Mentorship Brings Fluency

That is what mentorship is all about. A mentor helps you become fluent in the language that you want to speak. What I am going to teach you is something that you can use in every area of life - both spiritual and natural.

The mentorship process has been around since Adam and Eve. I do not think it was a good idea for Eve to receive mentorship from the serpent, but it is a good picture of what not to pick in a mentor. It is always a bad idea to follow a snake!

From the beginning of time that is the best way that humans have learned to do what they do. Look at your experience as you reached out to God, tried as hard as you could to do right and to study.

Then someone else came along and helped you to connect the dots. Although you learned a lot on your own, you still needed a mentor to come and sew all of those things together.

## My Personal Experience

You have probably also experienced that not everyone that calls themselves a mentor is a mentor. Having been on both sides of the spectrum, I want to share a bit of my experience on being a disciple and being a mentor.

When Jesus ascended, He said, "Go and make disciples of all nations." He did not do a big song and dance about it. He assumed that everyone there would go and do it. It is more natural than you realize to take the things that you have and pass them on to others.

I saw this with my son when he was around four years old. His sister, Ruby, was twelve at the time and when I asked him to do something I could see that Ruby had mentored him very well. I would say, "Michael, pick that toy up."

"Ugh."

"Michael, pick it up."

Flinging hands in the air with rolled eyes, "Fine... I'll do it."

Ruby definitely mentored him because he said and did the exact things that she would. From the very beginning, whether you have been born again for one day or for twenty years, God created us to take the portion that we have and pass it on.

I even saw Michael with a one year old friend, Mark. He sure mentored him in some things. Now, they were not very good things, and when I saw the two of them sneaking cookies from the kitchen I was well aware of a mentorship principle at play.

This is a natural process that has been forged in us since birth.

### Animals vs. Humans

Things are a little different for animals. Animals have instinct, but we have the ability to take what God has given us and impart it to others. Now, how you impart to others makes all the difference in the world.

 Humans are born to mentor.

## General Guidelines

I will start with some simple points of what to remember. Further along in the book I will take these points and expand on them more. So consider this a broad introduction to the subject to get you "up and running" with mentoring right away.

There is a lot in the Church about mentorship. There are many teachings on it and there is a lot of misunderstanding on it as well.

## 1. Mentor in One Area at a Time

Firstly, you only mentor someone or receive mentorship in one thing at a time. When that friend taught me German, she did not teach me German, French and Spanish all at the same time.

I would not have learned very much if that was the case. I learned just one language because that is all that I could take at a time. Sure, after that I could have also learned Spanish, but not at the same time.

It would have been too confusing. It is the same in a mentorship relationship. You can only be mentored in one thing at a time and there has to be a goal to reach.

I often hear people say that someone is their mentor. I ask them, "What are they mentoring you in?"

"They are just my mentor."

"What are they teaching or mentoring you in?"

"They teach me the Word, they teach me how to pray and they teach me how to be a good Christian."

"No this person is not your mentor. They sound like your pastor!"

We are not talking about parenting or pastoring here. We are talking about mentorship. If you are going to be mentored into something, then there has to be something that you are being mentored in, right?

## 2. There Must be a Goal

If you are going to be training or mentoring someone else, there needs to be a goal and a purpose. You cannot simply circle the airport and never land. Otherwise, it is exhausting and how do you know when it is time to leave?

How do you know if you should continue or not? Think about any mentorship relationship you have had or are in right now. What is the purpose? Do you know where you are going or what you are receiving?

 Write this down: What is the goal of this relationship?

This way, if something comes up that is wrong you can recognize it because it is clear that it is not helping you to reach the goal ahead.

I think people throw the word "mentor" around too casually.

They say, "I like this guy, he is my mentor." No. Mentorship is very specific. As God raises you up to impart to others, you better be sure that you know what you are giving them, how you are giving it to them and when it has come to its completion.

If you were at a job and someone was training you into a position, it is common knowledge that there is going to come a time when that training will be finished and you will be released into that position.

### The Christian Standard

Why should it be any different in the Church? Why do we see this wishy-washy stuff where everyone has a "mentor"? It is probably because it sounds cool.

It sounds really impressive if you say, "Do you know Prophet 'so and so' that has that huge church? They are my mentor."

Of course, that "mentor" does not even know their name, but they like to say it anyway because it sounds so great. No. He simply teaches you and if you are in his church, then he is your pastor. That does not make someone your mentor.

When you start looking at this subject from this perspective, you start seeing what a responsibility mentorship really is. It is not a game. It is not something that you can decide to pick up one day and say, "This seems cool. I am going to mentor someone."

## 3. You Can Only Take a Disciple to Where you Have Been

You better know what you are doing, what you are talking about and you better have lived whatever you are teaching. Here is the reality. You cannot mentor someone into something that you have never lived yourself.

It would not have been such a great idea for someone that speaks Italian to teach me German. I would have been even more messed up than before. Mentorship is very specific. If you have done any of our Fivefold Ministry School courses, then you are familiar with our stand on this as a ministry.

Because I have lived what I am teaching others, it gives me the courage to mentor effectively. Only when you have "been there" will you find the following phrases flow out of your mouth when dealing with a disciple,

"I am challenging you strongly on this point!"

"You need to die to your flesh because of this."

"I am going to brush past all of the political correctness because I am not going to meddle in your personal life or the areas that do not count!"

"God is calling you to this ministry and because of that, you need to get rid of this, this and that. Otherwise, forget it."

Having "lived it" gives you courage to be bold.

I can be bold because I have walked the road ahead of them. As a trainer, it gives me, the confidence to know that I can speak for God directly because I know where I am taking that person.

### Brings Security

Also, the person that I am leading can feel secure on the road they are walking. Perhaps, this is some of the struggle that you have had in mentorship relationships. Perhaps, you have tried to take someone under your wing and it never went anywhere.

Now you know why. You never took them anywhere. That is why it never went anywhere. You were thinking, "Ok. Let's see where this leads." If you do not know where it is leading in the beginning, then do not even start.

It is like saying, "I know I have never been to California, but let's just follow this road and see where it leads." You can end up in Mexico! I have seen it happen (figuratively and literally!) You can end up on the other side of the border if you do not know where you are going.

Did you get a GPS or an address for your destination or did you think that you would just jump in the car and see where this road takes you? Then, you wonder why you keep hitting walls and ditches.

You keep getting yourself into relationships that do not work. Both you and your disciple end up disappointed because both of you go into this relationship with different expectations and it does not work out.

Then you think that they are just rebellious and they do not want to submit. On the other side of the coin they think that you are just a dominating leader. No, the truth is that they are not connecting with you because there was no clear guideline given for what this mentorship is about and where it is going.

You both need to know what it should look like when it is time for this relationship to end. We need security and we need to know that there is a purpose for all of this death. We need to know that there is a reason for all of this travail.

I bet that is why you started searching. You can take the death, handle the correction and push through as long as you know there is a purpose for it. If you know that there is a goal at the end of this road, then it will be ok.

## 4. Plot out the Course

When God calls you to mentor someone, it is for you to plot that course so that they have hope. As ministers, we are called to bring hope to the body of

Christ. If you are in such a relationship, you need to ask yourself what your hope is.

What is the vision ahead? If you do not know, you are just wandering around and you are destined for discouragement. You are going to get discouraged with the Lord because He led you there, opened the door and everything is going wrong.

Things seem discouraging because you did not keep your eye on the goal. You never had a goal in the first place. Get the goal in mind and then the road that you have traveled will make so much sense.

It is not easy to be a disciple. I have had the privilege of being on both sides of this equation. I grew up a pastor's kid. When the Lord originally gave me my call, I learned under my father.

### Learning to be a Disciple

I learned how to be a servant and a disciple. My husband and I were under his ministry for 14 years. We pushed through and I thought that it would be like that forever.

It got to the point where that was my home. It was great. My father took the load and I could stand up and be the "hot shot" prophet. I could look cool, say what I wanted and he took the brunt of it.

I came to a point where I was content with being a spiritual child and a disciple for the rest of my life. Have you ever taken over the boss' position when they left? Have you perhaps taken over the church meeting when the senior pastor went on holiday?

Their job looks so easy. In fact, you can give a list of things they could do to do their job better. I had such a list. I thought, "If I was the pastor, I would do this, this and this. You can improve here and you can try this."

There came a time in my life when the Lord said, "You have learned to be a disciple, a child and a servant. Now, it is time to swap the tables a bit. You become the mentor, spiritual parent and leader."

## The Weight of Responsibility

I could flow in the gifts of the Spirit, I could preach and I could do all "the stuff". However, no one ever tells you about the load of responsibility that you carry as a mentor and leader.

Apostle Paul goes through this long list in 2 Corinthians 11 of the price that he has paid for the call of God on his life. He was persecuted and nearly killed, but he says that out of all these persecutions that nothing compared to the weight of the churches.

I thought, "The weight of the churches? What is this guy talking about?" I definitely know now. There comes a heavy weight of responsibility with your position and I will not let you out of it. If you have a little thought in your mind of one day becoming a leader in the body of Christ, get ready for it.

It will be a great weight to carry and it should be a weight. It should rest on your shoulders and you should take responsibility because if those under you fail, it is your responsibility before God.

 A godly mentor finds his strength on his face before the Father.

Paul knew that and that is why he was on his face before the Father carrying the weight. He knew that if he failed, it would mean those under him would fail and if those under him failed, it meant that he failed.

If we can take on that responsibility as leaders, it enables the Holy Spirit to work through us. We will always be weak and foolish. We will always need and want more. We will always be poor, hungry and thirsty because we know that we have to carry this load of responsibility.

If you have the opportunity to be a disciple first, take it, learn and rest. The greatest king that ever lived, King David, started out as a little shepherd boy disciple. Then we have "hot shot" Saul. What discipleship did he go through?

He was tall, handsome and had it all together. He looked like a king. He was anointed out of nowhere. They had to go and look for him. They put him on the throne overnight.

What kind of king did he make? The first time pressure came and God said, "Submit." He went off and did his own thing. He had not learned to serve or follow.

### David or Saul?

Do you really think David liked what Saul did to him?

Do you think that David agreed with how Saul did things? No. They did not have the same heart. However, David submitted to a point of calling him father and even when Saul tried to kill him, David said, "My father, why do you persecute me?"

He was nothing and that "nothing" became the mightiest king that Israel ever knew. He was in the bloodline of Christ. Why? It was because he knew what it was like to be a disciple.

# CHAPTER 02:
# Guidelines to Discipleship

Being a disciple to another person is the starting point to learning to be a true disciple of Jesus Christ. Many want to skip to "the mentor part" and be the leader. I am telling you now, the type of disciple you are will decide on the type of mentor you will become.

As much as you learn to serve, submit and bite your tongue when you do not want to, when you finally stand as the leader, you will understand those that are following you. Plus, you will have the Lord's grace, humility and passionate love to stand in confidence.

## The Price

I say to my team often, "I do not ask you to do anything that I am not prepared to do myself. If I am prepared to pay this price, then I expect it of you too." Can you say the same in your own life right now?

Do you expect of others things that you are not prepared to do yourself? It starts with understanding the disciple. You need to understand what it is like to be a servant. Being a disciple is like going through fitness training.

## 1. Submitting to Servant hood

It is like having a fitness trainer pushing you to your limits. I am not the athletic type, but when you become a disciple it is much like submitting yourself to a fitness trainer. Now, if you are someone like me that does not like being pushed, it can be difficult.

They are going to tell you to get your butt out of bed at six o'clock in the morning to go on a run. It is challenging. It challenges your flesh when God calls you to a discipleship relationship.

You think it is going to be so wonderful at the beginning. You think you are going to shop together, share your hearts, pray together and they are going to be your best friend. You think that whenever you have a problem you will be able to go to your mentor and they will be there when you are down and encourage you all the time.

## 2. Submitting to Pressure

Then the rest of the time, you can do whatever you want. No - When you sign up for mentorship, you sign on the dotted line that says, "I give you permission to push me to my spiritual limit."

Some of the ladies at our center, experienced this a while back. They said to my daughter Jessica, "We are going to go on a run at six o'clock every morning." (Why they decided to do that is still beyond my comprehension... I have decided that it was prophetic deception.)

So, anyway they decided that it would be fun to have this early morning run before starting the day. So, off they went on the first morning at six o'clock.

The next morning, Jess woke up and sat in the lounge waiting and wondering where the other ladies were. After a half hour, Jess brought them coffee and told them to get up. They slowly moved around and went off for their run.

A few days passed. One of the ladies came to me and said, "It started off with us asking Jess if she wanted to join us. This evening, Jess asked us if we were going to join her. She is killing my flesh!

She comes to my room every morning at six o'clock with a cup of coffee and a smile. Then, she tells me that it is time to run. My flesh is screaming."

This people, is what discipleship is about.

## 3. Not on Your Terms

It does not happen on your terms. Yet, you do start the process. You come up with this grand idea that it would be great to rise up and be a prophet or a success in your field. Then, someone comes to your door and says, "Get out of bed. Let's run!"

You have not even had your first cup of coffee yet.

You just want to die. Each training is different, but in prophetic training you are going to hear things like,

"This word is a deception."

"You are too loud."

"You are too arrogant."

"You are too proud."

Then you are going to think, "Lord, these dominating leaders are getting on my nerves."

You are the one that jumped into this relationship and signed on the dotted line. Do not complain when they are dragging you out of bed now at six o'clock in the morning. Stop flinching.

People pay a lot of money to have a fitness trainer. Can you imagine someone saying to their friends, "Can you believe that he made me do aerobics? What was my trainer thinking?!" Your friends will think, "Is that not what you hired him for?"

## 4. Remember Why You Signed Up - You Need Help

People get fitness trainers because they do not have the will power to push themselves. The reality is that if you were where you wanted to be in life, you would not need a mentor. That goes for anything in life, spiritual or natural.

If you had already reached your goal, then you would not need a mentor. So, do not flinch when you get a mentor and they start pushing you. You are not the person that you need to be in order to accomplish the task that God needs you to do.

If you were, you would already be accomplishing that task, wouldn't you? What is your vision and calling? Why are you not achieving the fullness of it right now? I am sure that you have many excuses.

### *What is Your Excuse?*

Everyone has an excuse, which is yours?

"The timing is just not right."

"It is the pastor's fault – he will not promote me."

"People do not receive me because I am a woman."

"People do not receive me because of my race."

"My language skills are the problem."

… The list is endless.

The truth is that you are not the person that you need to be in order to accomplish the vision that needs to be accomplished. That vision and calling needs a certain kind of person and you are not there yet.

> If you are not experiencing success, then who you are needs to change.

## 5. Dealing with Character Flaws

That is what the blessing of discipleship is about. It is about someone coming to you and saying, "Do you know that you have a mole on your nose? Get rid of it. Do you know that you come across arrogant? Deal with it."

We go through life not realizing that we have these character flaws. We do not realize that there are many things standing in our way. When we finally do find someone that has been along the way, you need to realize that they know a thing or two.

That is why they are where they are today. They have something that you do not. They know something that you do not. Yet, pride gets in the way because it means admitting that someone else knows something that you do not.

Many people just want a mentor's knowledge. If all you want is my knowledge, then buy my book or enroll in one of our courses. You do not need mentorship. Go read our free articles online.

If you think that all you need is knowledge to get you where you need to go, then help yourself. I also know that if I get up at six o'clock every morning and run that I will look very good, but the reality is that I do not have the will power, interest or care to do that.

However, there may come a time in my life where I might feel that I need to do that. I know that if that time comes, I will need help. I will need someone to push me when I cannot push myself.

### Discovering Your Inner Diamond

We like our comfort zones. We like to slip back into the old things and feel good and not have people tell us when things are wrong. Yet, sometimes we need people to tell us that things are wrong.

We need people to smooth those rough edges in our lives. There is a diamond in each one of us and there is a reason why it is not shining. You can get a rock out of the ground and see it with an untrained eye and think that it is just a rock.

However, if someone else sees it that has a trained eye for special rocks, they will see what you cannot. Then, a jeweler in his craft can cut that rock a piece at a time until it begins to shine.

You say, "What is wrong with me? I know that I am a diamond. I know that I have potential." This is true, but to the naked eye you are simply a rock. Others are not going to see the sparkle. You need the hand of a craftsman to come upon you.

### *You can Receive Directly from God*

You do not have to do that through mentorship. You can receive from God directly. However, how long did it take Moses to receive from God directly? It took him 40 years and then we have Saul who never got it right.

I am not saying that you cannot receive directly from God, but if you do it that way it takes longer. So, what is it going to be? If you want to do it yourself because you have forty years to kill and you do not care how long it takes, then hurray for you.

That is not the way that I like to do it. I want to get passed this mountain already and onto the next one. That is my nature. Bring on the hurts and pains and chisel the flaw off, so that I can shine and go onto the next treasure that God has waiting for me.

## Your Role as a Disciple

You get people who cry out to God saying, "Lord, change me!" Then someone comes with a corrective word and they say that the prophet does not know what they are talking about.

Then that person prays again and another prophet comes along with a word of correction and they think, "What is the problem with these people?"

They are not getting it. How many more times does God need to shout? They asked for change. Do they think that the diamond cutter is just going to come up and polish that rock by stroking it a bit?

No. He is going to take that rock and hit it on the flaw, not where it is comfortable. If you are being hit where it hurts and where it is uncomfortable, that is the point. If it is so uncomfortable, then you can be sure that it is the hand of God.

When someone comes with a word that is not from the Lord, it may make you angry, but it does not hit you in your heart. However, you also get those words that you hear and they make you want to die and repent on the spot.

Now, they hurt and sometimes you do not want to repent. Sometimes you hear them and you just want to shout, but you still know that they hit a sore spot. What are you going to do?

## 1. Learn the Power of Submission

As a disciple, it is for you to let it go and just submit. I tell my disciples all the time, "I do not promise you that it is going to be fair. Do not come to me expecting me to be a fair leader. However, I do promise that God will accomplish in you what He wants to do."

Sometimes, it is the unfair things that bring the worst out of us. These are usually the things that need to be brought to death. It is when someone is unfair to you that all the nasty stuff comes spurting out.

If I were to say nice things to you that make sense and are logical, then you would receive it and think that it is great. What about when someone is unjust, rude, arrogant and perhaps even in the flesh when they address you?

What is going to come out of you then? The greatest breakthroughs that I have seen in my disciples are not when I said the right thing, but when I said the wrong thing. I could have been completely wrong and maybe even in the flesh.

 I never promised that it would be fair!

However, when I see what comes out of them, I can tell that I have touched a flaw. When the Lord hits those flaws and He uses someone to bring the pressure, the quicker you let go the quicker you will be able to move on.

If you are wondering why you are not at your goal yet, you need to think on whether you have submitted or not. Have you received all that you need to?

### *Things Will Not Be Fair*

I am sure that ninety percent of the time it is not going to be fair. You can tell me all of your stories about how all the pastors mistreated you, but did you learn from those experiences that you should have learned?

Did you take the chisels and corrections even if they were wrong? Did you allow them to penetrate your heart and convict you? God can take care of you if you are being mistreated, but what came out of you?

When you were crushed, what came out of you? Did faith, hope and love come out? I do not think so. Sometimes God will put you in a specific situation or relationship just to bring out those nasty things.

It is not for the other person, but for you. God already knows the junk that is there. Why do you think He does it when He already knows what is there? He does it because you do not know what is there.

 God knows your flesh. Pressures expose your flesh so that you can see it for yourself.

## Understanding Pressure

That is the purpose of a mentorship relationship. You do not know that the junk is there because if you did, you would have dealt with it. If someone pointed out to you that you have a certain flaw, you would probably do all you could to change it.

It is because you do not know yourself what needs to be changed that you need a mentor. They can see what you cannot see. They have been down this way before you. Learn to follow through and submit to that pressure.

It is the greatest advice that I can give you. Do not think that because my mentor was my father that it made it any easier. I actually think that it made it harder. Who likes to be corrected by their dad?

We used to have huge fights. He said that no one ever gave him a harder time than me. I would fight with him for hours before I finally submitted.

Now when that happens to me with my team, I have a bit of grace. Before I get angry I think, "I did that too. I guess I better have some love with this one." There is nothing like having to deal with "yourself" to really bring you to death.

There were times when I really felt things were unjust. I felt that I gave my best and I tried hard, but I was still corrected. I would go and moan to the Lord and He would say, "Submit."

I would say, "Ah! I do not want to submit." Yet, I knew I had to. When you let go, it is like a veil that comes off your eyes and you see the truth. *"But when that which is perfect has come, then that which is in part will be done away." (1 Cor 13:10)*

### Pressures Are Seasonal

The pressures and conflicts that you are facing are only for a season. When that perfect gem comes out, this season will be done away with. The length of this season depends on how quickly you "get it" and pass through.

Another benefit of being a disciple is that the Lord will take you through these experiences until you "get it". However, being hardheaded means going around the same mountain again and again.

How many times have you been around the same mountain? How many times have you said, "Lord, why am I going through this again?"

That is why you need a mentor. They can tell you that you are going around this same mountain because you keep failing at the same point.

They can take you to that point again and then help you to climb the mountain instead of going around it. If you can see the balance of discipleship and its purpose, it makes you understand why the Lord always said, "Sit down, learn and submit. You may not understand right now or see what is going on, but once I have put my chisel on this final flaw, this diamond will shine."

When you get that this is producing something good in you, then you will start running toward the chisel instead of away from it.

My motto always was, "Let's get this on quickly."

I hated waking up in the morning and knowing that I was going through something.

I just felt a mess and wanted to break spiritual links with myself, but "myself" kept following me! I was just so annoyed with myself because I knew there was something that needed to be dealt with, but I did not know what it was.

This is where a mentor comes in handy. They walk up to you and say, "This is your problem." It hurts, but it is also a relief because we struggle so much and go around the same mountains again and again.

God has brought mentors into our lives to not only remove bad things, but also to impart and give us things.

## 2. Do Not Jump From Mentor to Mentor

Another thing to remember is that you should not hop around from mentor to mentor. A mentor can only disciple you in one thing at a time. Wherever God has you right now, you need to receive from there.

A disciple is meant to receive teaching and training. These are two very different processes. Teaching and instruction you receive from the pulpit. The training is when I get in your face and say, "Die already!"

That is like the fitness trainer knocking at your door and telling you to run. The teaching part is when you read the book about how cool it is to run and how you should do it. The teaching is the easy part.

### Learn and Train Together

When you submit to a mentor, you need to take the teaching and training side by side so that they can complement one another. You cannot take teaching from one source and training from another because when you receive the training you are not going to understand it.

You need to bring both together. When we take someone into a mentorship relationship, we say that they can only read our materials for that specific season of training.

 Your teaching and training should come from the same source.

We can do that because we are giving them direction as well as a clear goal and they know that when they come to the end of the road that it is over. I have very strict guidelines.

I will say, "When I am training you it is going to be for "this" purpose. This is the commitment that I am prepared to make to you and this is the commitment that I expect from you.

I expect that you read nothing but our teachings and materials because if I am going to train you in this area, I want you to be focused. When I come to bring the training, you better already have the principles because I do not have time to re-teach you.

I also do not want you pulling in information from everywhere else because I am trying to train you in a very specific area. It is just like the fitness world. There are many different things.

You have Zumba, Aerobics, Pilates, weight training and many more. You do not study about one type of fitness and then choose to do another. You stick to what you know. It would be foolish to study up on weight training and then attempt a Pilates class!

We had a woman come to us before and she said, "I eat the meat and spit out the bones."

She was saying that she takes what she wants here and she takes what she wants there. If that is what you want to do, then buy the books but forget about a mentorship relationship. You are wasting your time. When you just do a little here and a little there, you do not understand who you are, where you are going or what you are doing.

### Mixing Brings Confusion

You have so many "anointings" mixed up in your spirit and you still have not reached your goal. You think that taking a big chunk out of all these different teachings will speed you up.

You think that the more you take, the more you are going to be able to run. No. Actually, you are just going to be extremely weighed down. Stick to one. Pick one mentor and teacher and receive all that they have.

Mark could not follow Barnabas and Paul. He followed Paul and then he followed Barnabas and Paul said, "I will take on Silas now." Silas did not hang out with Peter and sometimes with Paul. They stuck together.

Timothy stuck with Paul. Each one had their own that they stuck with and received from. Was Paul greater than Peter? No, not at all. Was Peter greater than Paul? No, not at all.

When they decided who they were going to receive from, they stuck with that one teaching, anointing and training. As a result, they rose up very quickly. That is the exciting thing about having a mentor.

 Following through with one mentor ensures quick progress.

If you are prepared to pay the price and focus on that one person and receive all the teaching that they give you, know the goal ahead, submit to the training and allow them to challenge you. When you reach the goal you will both know it.

### *A Double Anointing*

It does not have to be painful and stressful. It truly can be like with Elijah and Elisha, who knew that the parting was coming any day. When Elijah did go Elisha could receive that double portion.

However, the reason you do not have the double portion is because you never stuck with somebody long enough to get it. Elisha did not go around snatching coats from everyone. He only took one.

Then God gave him double of that one. He received way more than Elijah had. God rewarded him beyond what Elijah had. That is the ultimate purpose of true mentorship. You are meant to take your team beyond what you have.

How can you do that if you are sipping here and there? When you look through your life and see the opportunities that God has given you, how many of them can you say you truly followed through with?

I am not saying that the people you worked with did not have a chip on their shoulders or did not have any issues. The Lord knows that we are all far from perfect. Yet, in your heart how many times did you truly follow through to the end? Not only when it was easy, but also when it was difficult?

## Dying in the Heat of Battle

Do you know when it is the best time to die? It is best to die in the heat of battle. It is best to die when the pressure is on you and you have the option to either run or to embrace it. How many times did you run?

Do not be frustrated if you are feeling a lack as a mentor. You are feeling that because you did not receive in the first place. Do not think that this only applies to human relationships.

If you are treating man like that, then you are treating God like that too. Many people say, "I will not submit to any man. I will submit to God." Saul had that same attitude as well.

King David could submit to both and Saul was hardly fair. Even when he had an opportunity to kill Saul with his bare hands, he said, "I will not put my hands on God's anointed. I will not touch him."

He submitted even when Saul was trying to kill him. God rewarded David for that. He did not have to fight for the throne like so many kings after him. God gave it to him. The princes of Judah and the whole of Israel came to him and handed him the kingdom.

He did not have to raise his hand and fight for it. God opened the way. When you have it right, you are confident in yourself and you know who you are. You do not have to fight for your calling. You just need to be the king that God has called you to be.

# CHAPTER 03:
# Mentorship – The Bottom Line

It is no secret. I am an expressive and when I want an answer to a question, I want it now! So before I get into the greater mechanics of mentorship, I am going to get you "up and running" with some practical guidelines to apply in your life right now.

In the chapters that follow I will be going into more detail in each of these points. For now though, write down each point and apply it to your life. They will help you set your course straight for the journey ahead.

So imagine me sitting across the way from you, explaining how I train my own disciples. As we talk as friend to friend, there are some things that I need to tell you about...

## Where to Begin

When I call someone to mentorship, I have a speech that I give them that is pretty much the same for each person. I have done quite a few of them, so I have shortened it a bit over the years.

I say to them, "I am calling you to this specific mentorship."

That is something that a lot of people in the Church do not understand. They do not understand that the mentor calls the disciple.

Elisha did not run up to Elijah, grab him by the scruff of the neck and say, "You are my mentor." No. Elijah came to Elisha and put his mantle upon him. It is always the mentor who calls the disciple.

When you get that order right, it brings rest. If you are going to call someone into that kind of relationship, you should know what you are going to mentor them in. Now, when you call them, there are a few things that you need to keep in mind.

## 1. Set the Stage

You need to let them know that you are calling them to mentorship in "this" specific area and that you are prepared to follow through with them. Let them know that they are going to get mad and spew at you. Tell them that there are going to be times when they will want to leave and that you will have some good fights.

However, let them know that you do not care how full of bitterness they are and how difficult it gets, you will not let go until God tells you to or unless they give up and go away.

You must let them know that you will be on their case. You will be there as a fire at their back to make sure that they do not give up. When they give up, you will not give up. When they do not want to get out of bed in the morning, you are going to be the fitness trainer that will not let it slide. You are going to follow through.

Until you have that clear line for mentorship, do not even start. If you are not prepared to follow through with someone from the first day, then do not even start. You are messing with their time and yours.

## 2. Commit to Follow Through

If you have not made the decision to follow through, the first time you get a backlash, you will say, "I won't take this. You can take your spewing and bitterness and leave."

How many people had the courage to follow through with you? Not when you were good, nice and putting on the "Sunday face", but when you were really a mess? That is what true mentorship is. It is having someone that will follow through with you.

As a mentor, you are the one that is meant to pull out all of the junk so that you can clean those wounds out and bring healing. Sometimes you need to bring pain so that they can realize that there is a hurt there and then you can bring healing to it.

After I have given my little speech and let them know what I will be prepared to do in the relationship, I tell them that I expect the same commitment from them. It is a two-way relationship.

Did Elijah expect anything less from Elisha? Elisha says, "I am going to go bury my family." Elijah said, "Cheers." If you are not prepared to commit to me after I have decided to commit to you, then you can go away and have a good life.

So Elisha took his oxen and slaughtered them and he broke his cart. He paid the same price that Elijah was prepared to pay. He let that life go and burned his bridges.

Once that has taken place, you now have a mentor-disciple relationship.

I am not afraid to be a little arrogant and bold because if I am going to mentor someone I am not going to give them one little piece here and there. I am going to give them everything and they better be willing to pay the price that I was willing to pay.

"I do not need you to pay a bigger price. I do not need you to do or be more. I just want you to meet me at the same level. If I am prepared to follow through with you, are you prepared to follow through with me?

When I tell you I expect submission from you that does not mean that you should not say anything. I want you to speak and say what you should and should not. I want you to be real with me. Then I know what is there and what we need to work on.

You are going to read my teachings and nothing else because I want you to know these principles so that when I come to you and tell you what you need to deal with, you know what I am talking about."

## 3. Give Them a Goal

It is a bit harsh, eh? It may be, but it gives us a sense of security. I would rather have someone be direct and strict than to have someone that says, "Let's see what happens today. Let's see where the wind carries us."

I want to know when I am going to get to the goal. I do not want to hear, "We will see how it goes." We have so many mentors that just tell people to hang out with them for a bit and come around when they have meetings and then they will see how the Lord leads.

Where does the Lord lead in times like this? It seems that He is leading you around in circles because nothing happens. God does not lead in circles. He has a clear goal for your life.

### The Greatest Show of Love

If you are working with someone, you need to know what the goal is before you open your mouth and call them into a mentorship relationship. You need to first be prepared to follow through.

I think that following through with someone is the greatest love that we can ever show one another. That is why I love the Lord so much. It is not because He pats me on the back when I do well.

I love Him because when I am a complete mess and I have failed Him miserably, He still chooses in His grace, to pick me up, use me and pour His anointing through me.

Even if I have just disappointed Him and I feel that I have truly let Him down, this is when He shows up in my life the most.

A sign that you found the right mentor is that you found someone to follow through with you no matter what.

He follows through with me. He never lets go when I let go. Even when I ran away from Him and wanted nothing to do with Him, I looked back and I saw Him chasing me. He never let go.

That is why I adore Him and that is why I will pay any price for Him. It is not because I am so great. It is because He is so great and He was there when I did not deserve it. He followed through with me.

## 4. The Holy Spirit Trains

As a mentor, God calls you to represent Christ to His people. This means that you are going to have to follow through with people that He brings to you. It means that you are going to have to stand in His image.

The most exciting part of all in being a mentor is that you are not the person training and shaping them. You are just the trainer. You did not make the weights or set this up. The Holy Spirit is the person doing the work.

You are just there to help them recognize what the Holy Spirit is doing in their life. Some of the conversations will sound like this, "You are so silly. Can you not see that 'this' is happening right now? Can't you see that the Lord is trying to get your attention?"

### The Little Secret

That is what a mentor is there for. I started mentoring the prophets when we started our first prophetic school in 1999. I thought that I was going to be the best mentor and trainer in the world.

I worked so hard. I invested, poured out, ministered and I did not even stop on holidays. I was the person that was going to change and shape people's lives. I was going to do so much that I forgot that it was God that was going to do the work and I was just along for the ride.

One day I got a revelation. It hit me that they are God's children and not mine. It is for God to change them, not me. When that revelation hits you, it shakes your foundation.

You know it already in your head, but when it really sinks into your spirit it takes the pressure off you.

It is for the Holy Spirit to arrange the circumstances in their lives. There will be times when your disciples will not submit to you and you will think, "I have invested all of this time and they are never going to come right. Where did I fail? What could I have said or done?"

Then you will go before the Lord and He will say, "Have you forgotten that they are my child? Have you forgotten that they are in the palm of my hand, not yours? Put them into my hands and let me do the work."

When those difficult times come, do not forget that God is able to get through to them. God is able to reach through to them. Get yourself out of the way. Some of the greatest chisels that I have ever given were by just backing off.

So let's say you have a disciple and you give them a correction and they fly off the handle. They spew and tell you how dominating you are. In moments like this you just have to say, "Ok. I gave it to you the easy way."

## God's Pattern for Correction

There is a specific way God corrects. He uses your mentor first, then He moves onto the people that are closest to you after that. That may be your family, spouse or the church you are in. The same thing that your mentor said will come back at you again through another vessel.

Then if you do not receive it from any of those avenues, pressures will start coming upon you from the world.

When they came to break the legs of the three on the cross, Jesus was already dead. He did not need His legs broken.

# The Leg-Breaking Experience

However, the two thieves were still kicking up and trying to survive, so they got their legs broken. Jesus simply let go and said, "It is finished." He surrendered. The others kicked up so that they could still breathe.

Therefore, the soldiers came to break their legs so that they could not kick up and continue to breathe. After having their legs broken they suffocated to death. That is what we call a leg breaking experience.

A leg breaking is when the Lord tells you to let something go through your mentor and you do not receive it. Then that same pressure will come at you again, but this time from the world. There will be sudden hard, natural pressures that will come at you.

You will get pressure at work and everywhere you are. They will continue to come again and again. When this happens, realize that the Lord is shouting at you and trying to get your attention. He is saying, "When are you going to listen?"

### God is in Control

So when you are mentoring someone, do not forget that you are not the one that has to change them. Some of the most powerful prayers that I have ever prayed were, "Father, I put this person into your hands. Lord, I have done what I can. I am here and I am waiting."

Then I will see a vision of them needing to pass through a river and I am standing on the other side. I will say, "Holy Spirit, it is for you to bring them through." I let them know that I am there for them and I am not budging. I am following through, but I let them do what they want until they come back to me.

After I pray, I sit back and wait. It does not take too long. When you have a mentor praying with spiritual authority, things happen quickly.

Your disciple will contact you and tell you all the things that have been happening and you will know that they hit the wall big time.

You can say, "Good. Can we now go back to what I addressed in you before? Can't you see that this is what God is trying to accomplish in you?"

Now is the time to take them through the problem and follow through with them.

However, there are times when you will need to back off. Just because you do not succeed with someone does not always mean that you failed. It could just mean that they are not yet ready to deal with that specific thing yet.

Let the Holy Spirit do what He does best. It is just important for you to not let go unless God says so. As a mentor there are times when you want to walk away from a difficult disciple and you want to say, "God, are you kidding me? I am letting you know that I want to let go and run away from this!"

It gets difficult sometimes. It is really challenging. Remember that God will not let you down. You are going to be triggering everyone. There are going to be times when you will be working with someone when suddenly these emotions and other stuff come at you out of nowhere.

They will be making great progress and you will think that they are ready to take off and do great things. Then you will say something and a volcano will suddenly erupt out of them. You will think, "Where did this come from?"

Of course the volcano is going to erupt all over you because you are the closest and you are the one that stuck your nose in there. So you will get all the junk. That is a part and parcel of being a mentor.

## 5. Do Not Make Things Personal

You are meant to pull that stuff out of them. You will even need to do it on purpose sometimes, so that they can deal with it. Also, remember that you cannot let their bitterness or things that they are going through become personal.

You have to realize that when you are working with people, you are going to trigger them to their father, mother and experiences from the past. When they are spewing at you, they are not really spewing at you.

You just happen to be the last link in their chain. This has probably happened to them many times in their lives and you are probably the only one that has said something about it and told them to work through it.

You are going to have to go back through the links in that chain and undo what has been done. A real mentor will have the courage to recognize and say something when their disciple says, "This always happens in my life. This person did it and that person did that."

That mentor will say, "Don't you see a pattern here? Let us go back and deal with that." However, if you have insecurities, a fear of man or failure, then you are going to take it personally when they spew at you.

Your own bitterness will even start coming up. After the first conflict you will want to give up. You need to be prepared to follow through. There is nothing more rewarding than working through those moments.

I tell my team to shout at me, to tell me to take a hike or tell me to jump off a cliff. I just want them to tell me something! Then I can see what lies inside. If you yell at me, I can see the junk that is there and then we can deal with it.

That is how we bring healing and change. After you are done reading this book, I would have left you with the responsibility of true leadership and mentorship. If you are not quite there yet, enjoy your time of discipleship.

### The Chisel Has It Hard

If you are a disciple then enjoy being the one to receive. This is a restful time, even though there are deaths and challenges. My husband, Craig, shares a lovely illustration for this.

He says, "As a trainer, God uses us as a chisel on the diamond. No one ever thinks about the hammer that hits the chisel into the diamond."

The chisel is getting it on both sides. You think that you have it tough being the diamond, but the chisel has a hard diamond in front and a hammer in the back.

It is not comfortable being a mentor. There is more pressure on you as a mentor than as a disciple because you are taking someone's life into your hands and you better know what you are doing.

If you do not hit that diamond where you are meant to, you will make it useless. You better know where you are hitting and you better have been discipled correctly. You better have risen up correctly and not as a "Saul".

How many lives were lost because of Saul's arrogance? His own son was lost because of his arrogance. He would not take the time to submit and listen to God. Do not make the same mistake. So enjoy your time of listening in your discipleship season.

 **Tools of the Trade**

## Identify your Role as a Disciple

We are disciples in many different areas of our lives. In our business, social and spiritual lives, we have mentors and we are disciples on many different levels. I want you to take some time right now and think about the areas of life where you are a disciple.

Think about where you are learning something specific.

1.  Where are you receiving from someone to get to a goal?

    It could be learning to cook from someone or being mentored into prophetic office.

2.  Where are you a disciple in your life right now?

3.  Are you receiving everything that you should while you are in this relationship?

Seasons do not last forever and if you do not receive what God has put you there to receive, then this season will pass and you will miss out.

Make sure that wherever God has placed you to receive that you receive everything you need. I thought that season of my life would last forever, but there came a time when God moved me on.

## Identify Your Role as a Mentor

1. Where are the areas in your life where you are being a mentor?

   You may not even realize it. My daughter, Ruby, mentors my son, Michael and she does not even realize it. Yet, it is so obvious looking on the outside.

   When he is getting dressed, she says, "You have to button your shirt like this and tie your shoes like that." It is a simple mentorship relationship. She is imparting to him what she has. In the same way, there are many in your life that you are teaching.

   It may simply be in your home. It started out for me with my children. You mentor people in so many areas without even realizing it. Don't think that one day you are going to be this great mentor. Instead realize that you already are a mentor.

   Perhaps you are not at a high level mentorship yet, but you just need to start in the relationships that you already have. As you excel in those, the Lord will take you higher and higher.

   You are not just going to go from the bottom all the way to the top. If God is training you to be a leader, you are going to start learning that in your home. It will start with your spouse and children.

   You will start learning to impart what you have before jumping into high level mentorship.

2. As a mentor, are you imparting everything that you have in that relationship?

3. If you are suddenly taken away, could they carry on without you?

   Whether it is your children, disciples or even someone at work, are you truly giving them the best opportunity so that God can remove you and they can still carry on? Are you giving them that vote of confidence?

4. What is the goal that you have given your disciples to follow?

   They may not be like you yet, but are you at least giving them a goal and letting them know that this is what the picture looks like at the end? You will work towards it together and you will see that there is a price on both ends.

## Read With Expectation

It may start off slowly, but there is an end goal. As you read through this book, I will be your mentor. Do not read through with preconceived ideas, but go through it expecting God to put His finger on certain things in you.

If you feel a flaw being hit in you as you read through this book, thank God because there are not many people in our lives that have the courage to open their mouths and tell us when we have a flaw.

Usually, the only people that do have the courage to do these things are people that do not like you very much. You have an opportunity to receive in this book. Allow the Lord to challenge you.

It is no fun getting up at six o'clock in the morning to go out for a run or to do a heavy workout. Yet, when you have done that workout and you wake up the next morning in pain, you are happy because you did something good for your body.

Yes, it may hurt, but it is good pain because you know that if you can keep it up you will get slimmer, fitter, faster and stronger. That pain means that something really happened and you really pushed yourself.

You are accomplishing something. You can rise up very quickly. You do not have to go around the same mountain anymore. I am giving you the shortcut. Know that with every shortcut there comes a price.

The price for shortcuts is to submit to corrections from the Lord, your mentor, fellow believers or even the world. Yet, if you can take those corrections and continue rising up, then you can move forward quickly.

If you look at my team, you will say, "Please explain to me how a sixteen year old can stand up and share with so much confidence?" It is because she knows how to "die already."

It is not because she knows how to stand up and be bold. It is because she knows how to let go. That is the power of Christ. It is no longer I that lives, but Christ that lives in me. John the Baptist said, *"He must increase, but I must decrease." (John 3:30)*

If you want to rise up quickly and walk in His power, then there needs to be less of you and more of Him. Let Him chisel away the flaws, the rock and the "you." Let Him bring the "me", the "my vision" and "my" everything to death.

Then let Him fill you with the latter rain. You just have the former. You just have a small drop. He will fill you with His desires and you must know that there is nothing small about God. His desires and ambitions for you are great.

> To walk in power is not about getting "more" but about "letting go"

He cannot even be contained in the heavens. There is something very freeing about letting go. If you want His power, it is not about getting more. It is about how much you let go.

God is calling you to let go. You are saying, "More Lord, more Lord." God is saying, "Less first. Then you will get more."

Receiving the anointing takes five minutes. It is letting go of the junk that takes longer.

When you are free of the junk it is so easy to take on more. When you let go of all those burdens, you will be able to run. The more will come. For now, let us get rid of all that junk that is there.

God will empower you once that has been done. It will be a quick work. Now, as I have spoken many things have come to mind. I do not want you to try and remember everything that you read.

## Your Personal Conviction

I want you to remember what God has pierced in your heart. Forget the fluff and the "blah, blah" that I have given you and concentrate on the points where you felt God putting His finger on something inside of you.

That point is the seed that God has planted into your heart. I do not want you to try so hard to receive everything that you read in this book. I want you to receive what God has for you.

There are many people that will read this book. Therefore, when I am writing this book I am jumping and hitting many different topics because God is speaking to many different people and meeting many different needs.

All you need to do is remember the points that God is addressing in you. If you are going to make any notes in your diary, just write down the points that strike your heart. Get your word and meditate on it.

Then you can say, "Holy Spirit, show and teach me more." I am just going to be used to plant a seed. He is going to take that seed and make it grow and add additional revelation to it.

## Prayer

> *"Thank you Holy Spirit. I ask that you take those seeds now and apply them to each heart. You know everyone that is reading this book and you know what level they are at and the struggles that they have gone through."*

> *I see someone trying to walk and they have lots of bungee cords around them. It has become so hard to walk. You know that you need to go forward, but there are many cords around you pulling you back.*

> *You think, "Lord, why does this walk have to be so difficult." It is just because you have all these things that you are holding onto. You have old wounds and experiences and you think that you have to hold onto them.*

> *There may be disappointments that you had with some people and you are holding onto them like a badge. You are saying, "This and that happened to me. That person said something terrible and this person said 'this'. I am not going to listen to anything they say. I am going to do what I need to do."*

> *Actually, you do not realize that your attitude is keeping you hooked onto that bondage and holding you back. Let it go. Forgive them. Whether they were right or wrong, it does not matter. Who cares if you were right and they were wrong? Let it go.*

*You need to realize that it is holding you back. I ask you, Holy Spirit, to reveal these things. Bring a conviction. Speak to them in dreams or however you need to. Bring back memories and people's faces to their minds.*

*There is so much baggage that needs to be let go of. There are many disappointments, hurts, lost opportunities, places where you failed, people that have let you down and you keep carrying all these things around.*

*The Lord wants to set you free. He wants to make you like King David and cause you to dance before the ark with such joy. He wants to take the load off you. Let go of your failure and your discouragement.*

*He whom the Son sets free is free indeed. Thank you, Holy Spirit, for unraveling these things and for bringing victory into each one's life in Jesus' name. Amen."*

# CHAPTER 04:
# Mentorship - What to Expect

Mentorship has been a big subject in the body of Christ for some time. Everyone has a mentor these days. At first glance it all sounds so simple - until the day when you try to mentor somebody for the first time!

In this book I will guide you through the process of mentorship one step at a time, and in so doing, impart all the years of my own experience to you.

I learned things the hard way and so I am here to help you avoid the pitfalls. You can learn from my mistakes and take advantage of my successes.

However, as in all things, there are just some lessons in life that you have to learn for yourself. I am sure you have already experienced some of this and learned a few things the hard way.

To make your mentorship journey easier from now on, I am here to give you a blueprint and share the shortcuts. I will teach you what to avoid and most importantly, I will share with you how to become the mentor God has called you to be.

This leads me to the first point that I want you to understand right from the beginning:

Mentorship is a natural ability that is learned.

## Mentorship 101

In Matthew, when the Lord ascended, He said to His disciples, *"Go therefore and make disciples of all the nations, baptizing them in the name of the Father and of the Son and of the Holy Spirit." (Matt 28:19)*

Now, just receiving the command does not make you a good mentor! So are you born with this gift? I have three daughters and not one of them looked like a good mentor when they were born. I could not say that they were born with a "gift" for mentorship.

Here is the reality - Mentorship is a naturalistic ability. It is not a spiritual gift. People are saying, "I have the gift of mentorship." Well, can you find that for me in the Word?

The Lord does not give out the "gift of mentorship". He gives out the gift of tongues, prophecy and the gift of discerning of spirits, but not mentorship. So I cannot lay hands on you and impart the gift of mentorship.

There is no such gift or spiritual ability – but there is such a natural ability. The good news is that this is something that anyone can learn. This is a natural process that takes place not only in the body of Christ, but all over the world.

## The Simplest Form of Mentorship

If you watch a cat with her kittens, you will see how she teaches her kittens her way of life. Is that not a form of mentorship? You see teachers teaching children their ABC's. Is that not mentorship?

You may join a big company and your boss will show you the ropes. That is mentorship.

Then we look at the spiritual aspects of our calling, aspects such as how to train people in the Word or one of the fivefold ministries. Now you may have all the spiritual ability, the anointing, the fire, the charisma and the power; however, until you are a good mentor you are not going to be able to impart those gifts, abilities and anointing to others.

Do not assume that just because you have all these abilities that they will make you a good mentor. Why? Because mentorship is a natural ability that is learned, it is not something that is imparted or dropped from the sky.

You can even desire it as much as you like, but until you learn to mentor, you will not be able to mentor. If you have been thinking, "I do not know what to do with the people God is sending to me for mentorship," do not feel ashamed.

## Failures of Spiritual Giants

The most powerful apostles, prophets, ministers and even revivalists did not know how to mentor. Take a look at all of the revivalists of the past. Tell me, how many of their movements are still alive today?

Who were their disciples? Who carried on the flame after they died? Not many did because they did not mentor anyone. Do you think that is bad? Read the New Testament and tell me who Apostle Matthew's disciple was.

Tell me who Phillip's disciple was. Even in the New Testament you will see that only a select few of the apostles speak of their spiritual sons, daughters and those that they mentored and passed their inheritance to.

We are talking about the fathers of the faith, those that founded the new church. It does not mean that just because you have a mandate, calling or a good ability that you are a good mentor.

Mentorship is not an instinct. On the other hand, this is good news because it means that anyone can learn to mentor. You can learn to mentor in both natural and spiritual things. In this chapter, I am going to concentrate more on mentoring in spiritual things.

### Internship is Essential

In our ministry we put together a concept of internship, which is basically taking all the students that have qualified, and then mentoring them by showing them the ropes. It is similar to what happens when you join a company and they teach you to do your job properly.

They will show you how to do the job the way that they do it and hopefully you become better, so that the company may grow. That is what we do in our ministry. We teach you how to do the work of the ministry.

Just because you have the anointing, does not mean that you know the basics of everyday ministry. "Knowing the stuff" and actually putting your hand to the plow with experience are two very different things.

## Elijah and Elisha

Why do you think it took Elisha so long to rise up into office? He followed in the footsteps of Elijah for many years before he took over. He needed to learn how to wash hands, be a servant and gain experience. It was more than just the anointing that he needed.

Before you can pass on what you have to others, you need to learn a few things. If I had to paint a really good picture of what mentorship is about, I would say it is like being a surrogate parent.

 Be a good mentor to qualify as a spiritual parent.

## Surrogate Parenting

I had an experience of being a surrogate parent a long time ago at the age of 14 when my mother left us. I had two younger sisters and my father had to work. So I came home and there were things that just needed to be done.

I did not wake up one morning and say, "I am going to take charge and do what I have to do." No. It was thrust upon me. I learned to cook, to take care of the house and to care for my sisters to the best of my ability at that age.

Unfortunately, I had not fully matured yet. I did not know everything that there was to know about life. I could only take my sisters as far as where I was, which was very limited. However, the Lord was gracious and He brought my stepmom, into our lives.

She then stepped in as the true mother and took over the responsibility that I had been carrying for that short while. I had been like a surrogate parent in the home. I had taken care of the stuff and done little things, but I was not the real Mom.

I was simply holding the reigns for a little while, filling the post and helping them through that transition. Yet, when my stepmom stepped in, I could let go. I was only the surrogate parent. She was the real thing.

If you have heard any of our teachings on spiritual parenting, you know that there are three main relationships you can have in your spiritual life. You can have a mentor, a spiritual father and a spiritual mother.

As a mentor, you prepare a person for spiritual parenting. A lot of the functions that you fulfill will seem similar to those of a spiritual parent.

However, just because you are doing those jobs, does not necessarily mean that you are a spiritual parent. So I want you to lower your sights a bit, because until you have learned to be a proper mentor, you will not qualify to be a spiritual parent.

## Mentorship Requirements

Until you know how to mentor properly, you will not be able to go to the next level. Those of you that are reading this that are at a higher level of ministry, I want to bring you down a bit.

I want you to learn this level first, because this is your foundation. Let's start with some practicalities. Where do you start? This sounds very simplistic, but stick with me.

Before even starting a mentorship relationship, make sure that you have the following things sorted out.

## 1st Requirement. What do You Have to Give?

I am not going to mentor someone in woodworking or handcraft. Can you guess why? There is a very good reason. I have never picked up a circular saw in my life. I have never touched a power tool.

So it would be very stupid of me to try and mentor someone in something that I do not even have a clue about.

So think about it for a moment. What abilities do you have? What natural and what spiritual abilities do you have? What gifts has God given you? Take a look because if you mentor someone, it will be in one of these things.

You are going to impart what you have. There is a lot of need in the body of Christ right now. However, if you are having serious problems in your marriage, you are not going to mentor someone in their marriage!

How are you going to counsel someone in their marriage, when you do not even have this strength in your own life? You are going to have to mentor in your own abilities. You cannot mentor in the unknown. What can you impart if you do not have anything?

## 2nd Requirement. There Must be Purpose

The first thing you need to realize when the Lord leads you to mentor someone is what you are mentoring them in. Do not just say, "I am mentoring this person." What are you mentoring them in?

Do not just mentor someone in "stuff". You say, "The person I am mentoring is doing great." They are doing great in what? You cannot say, "They are doing great in... 'Stuff'." No, mentorship is very specific.

Mentorship is specific. Only one thing at a time.

You need a track to run on. If you do not even have a track to run on, then where are they going to find a track to run on? You have to give them something to work with.

What are your strengths and abilities? Concentrate on those things. Then also know that when you take on a disciple, they are not going to take on all of your strengths and abilities. They will only take on the strength of what you are mentoring them in.

A person may have many mentors. Mentoring is specific. If I am mentoring someone in our fivefold ministry school, I am not going to mentor them in both the pastoral and the apostolic offices at the same time.

I am more than likely going to mentor them in the pastoral first and then once they have reached that office, they may even go away for a while. However, if they come back and they are ready for the next level, I can then mentor them in the apostolic.

They can also choose to go somewhere else and be mentored by someone else. The Lord may even send them to another mentor.

You can only mentor someone in one of your abilities at a time. This helps you to focus.

There will be times when you will be working with someone and they will get off track into other things, and you will have to bring them back to the focus on what is important at that moment. You will have to keep them focused on what you are mentoring them in.

### Natural vs. Spiritual Mentorship

It is very common to have a mentor in something spiritual and another mentor in something natural at the same time. This can work - as long as they do not clash.

For example: I receive mentorship from an apostle for a new ministry office that the Lord is putting me in. At the same time someone at work is mentoring me in graphic design.

You see, your mentor at work mentors you in naturalist things because that is a strength that she has. She doesn't try to mentor you in all of the spiritual gifts. She just takes the natural abilities that she has and imparts them to you.

It is the same with the apostle. He takes the spiritual ability that he has and imparts it to you. It is very clear.

What are your strengths? With that in mind, you are now ready to impart what God has given you.

# 3rd Requirement – Know Your Disciple

You will start by getting to know the person that you are mentoring. Now that you have a disciple, it is not always important that they know everything about you. However, it is very important that you get to know everything about them.

This training is all about them. That is why it is so important that if you have any needs that you get them met in the Lord, or find your own mentor or spiritual parent to get those needs dealt with.

 Mentorship is 100% give!

When it comes to mentorship, it is one hundred percent give for you, whereas for them it is one hundred percent take. It is not a give-and-take relationship. You give one hundred percent and they take one hundred percent. That is the way it works.

It is not an attitude of, "I did you a favor so now you do me a favor." You cannot expect them to meet your needs or help you out. You are the mentor.

### No Room for Neediness

Think about it. When you have a new born baby in the house, it means one hundred percent give.

As a Mom you are breast-feeding, diaper changing, taking care of the laundry and making sure the house does not fall apart. The child on the other hand is only drinking, crying, and doing whatever they want to do. That is a good picture of mentorship.

If you have any needs that have not been taken care of, then now is a good time to take care of them. Why is that? It is because until you have heard their story, how will you know where to help them?

It does not mean that because you have this great ability that they are automatically going to pick it up. You need to know where their weak points and abilities are. You need to know those things, so you can take what you have and impart it to them.

### Get Them Talking

So the first thing that you need to do is sit them down and get them to talk about themselves. From your side, only ask questions. They do not want to hear your story anyway!

If they do ask a question, it is only so that they can talk about themselves again. Get them to talk. The biggest mistake that you can make is to sit someone down and give them an hour long lecture on mentorship.

Forget it. Get them to talk first. Ask them personal questions. Ask them about their upbringing and their relationship with their parents and siblings. Start gathering information and you will be surprised at how much you can find out by simply taking the time to ask them questions.

Ask them what burns in them for ministry. Ask them where they were born and what they studied. Do you really know those things about the people that you work with? You should be asking them if they are married.

You should be asking them what their relationship with their spouse is like and how long they have been married. Do you know these things? Knowing these things will give you a very good picture of where they are coming from and you will be able to meet their need.

Every disciple is different. Just because you have this ability does not mean that they are automatically going to learn to do what you do.

## 4th Requirement: Disciple Must Admire You

For someone to receive what you have, they need to admire you. So first impressions do count. Do not decide to disciple someone that has a bitterness issue with you and will not give you the time of day.

You are wasting your time. You need to disciple those that admire you; because when they admire you, they will receive from you instantly. It is important that the disciple knows how important their mentor is and what a special person they are.

Sometimes you hear, "I just want to be humble. I do not want to exalt myself or puff myself up."

Well, if you do not do that, then they are not going to admire you or receive from you. Trust me... if they admire you they will receive quickly.

They will imitate you without you having to say, "Imitate me". You are trying not to be like the dominating leaders out there, but here is the key... people admire them. They admire those dominating leaders. The question is, do they admire you?

If they do not admire you, it is not because you are humble – it is because you are insecure. You are not being humble. You are actually being arrogant by thinking that you are better than those "dominating" leaders.

If you do not give them something to admire, then they will never change. They will continue to run after the dominating leaders that do put on that image. So why don't you put on something different?

## Standing in Authority

How about putting on the image of Christ, putting those insecurities in the closet and rising up instead? Be the leader that God has called you to be instead of whimpering around all the time.

So what if you are a failure? God has called the weak and foolish. You are weak, foolish and pathetic. I know that and you know that - but they do not need to know that. God has delegated His authority to you and His delegated authority is greater than your natural authority.

King Ahasuerus placed Haman as second in command and everyone had to bow. The man was evil. We know that. We read the Word and we see what he wanted to do to the Jews. However, he had delegated authority that covered all his character flaws.

Later we read how Mordecai was placed in his position and rose up from being spat on to being bowed down to. Why? Did he suddenly become a better person? Nope, he was given authority! (Esther 8:2)

You know something. You and I stand together today in delegated authority from the King of all kings. I do not care how much weakness and insecurity you have. I stand in delegated authority and when I speak to you under that delegated authority, you better listen.

You better listen because it is not me that is speaking. Do not think that you are humble by holding back. You are just being arrogant, selfish and insecure. You are too afraid to stand up in authority in case of rejection. That is a selfish and childish attitude!

## Time to Be Counted

It is time to stand up in the authority that God has given you. If God, the creator of the Universe, can trust you, then you can certainly trust yourself. If He has delegated that authority to you then He will back you even in your mistakes.

Do you understand? This is not about how good, bad or anointed you are. I am dealing very strongly with the naturalistic side right now.

If you do not stand up and be that image of Christ, people will not admire you and so they will not receive the pattern that God has given you. They will also not receive the anointing and abilities that you have.

If you are too weak then no one is going to follow or admire you. They will continue to follow the "big guy" that dominates them. On one hand the people complain and on the other they imitate him exactly.

You say, "I do not know what the Church is coming to." You can sit there wringing your hands all you like, but until you become a leader with the heart of Christ, you will never change the Church.

## It's Worth It

So stop complaining and rise up. Yes, you will rise up in the flesh sometimes and get it all wrong, but your failure means nothing if they receive just an ounce of the power that God has given you.

Is that not what matters? Is the pattern, anointing and love not what really matters? If you are afraid because of one little mistake, then the body of Christ loses out on such an awesome inheritance and treasure.

Your sins and your failures are not important to God - your heart is. Do not be afraid to let others admire you. If you are under covering, and you walk out of line, then soon enough you will be brought back into line.

Do not worry about that right now though. The Lord is gracious. He can exalt and humble. However, at least take a step and give out what you have.

# CHAPTER 05:
# Start Here

## Step 1: Breaking Down Walls

*Proverbs 28:23 He who rebukes a man will find more favor afterward than he who flatters with the tongue.*

You have a disciple, you have heard their life story and you have everything together. Where do you start? Here is the first problem. Most people have difficulty opening their hearts to others.

It is not uncommon to find people like this. Even with a desperate need for acceptance, many people will battle to open up and to feel comfortable around you.

So if you have a meeting with them, then for the first meeting you should not talk about ministry stuff, because you want them to let their guard down a little.

You just need to get to know them as a person. Talk a lot. Make yourself friendly and approachable. Please memorize these two words... "I understand". Ask them questions and get them to talk.

 Memorize these two words: "I understand!"

By the second or third meeting you may find that they still have not opened up their heart to you. This is when the chisel will have to come out, because until you get to the heart of the matter, you will have to break down the walls.

## Using the Chisel

This is where you really have to stand in your authority and be straight with them. If they are not opening up you will need to say, "You have put up walls with me. I want you to put them down." It is really simple.

Say, "I understand that there are a lot of hurts and that you are being cautious, but until you let the walls down, let me in and show me the real you, I am afraid I cannot work with you."

That may do it. However, you do get those that will try to worm around it, or outright disagree with you. They will say, "I am being very open." What should your response be in this situation?

You cannot walk on eggshells and just sit there thinking, "Ok there is nothing I can do." They have to admire you. Do not excuse yourself.

If you say that they are putting up walls, then they are. I do not care how they feel. You can say, "You may not feel like you are putting up walls, but me and everyone else in the world can feel those walls. So you are the one with the problem.

If I am seeing them, then everyone else is too and until you are prepared to look at them, there is nothing that I can do with you. Come back when you are ready."

If they admire you, they will either go away or crack down the middle and then you will have something to work with. Until you bring them to a place of being open to receive from you, they won't receive any correction or love you give them.

### Nice People are not Always... Nice

The problem is that the walls are the thickest with the "nice" people. It is easy to spot the walls when a big, hard guy comes to you. Yet, in my experience those are the easy ones. You say one or two words and they melt like chocolate left in your glove compartment.

It is the ones that appear open and tell you how they are honored to have you in their life, that have the biggest walls. They tell you that they have been waiting for a mentor and that they are going to receive and do everything you say.

They give such a nice performance for everyone that people never see the real them. If you are fooled by that flattery, then you will never address it.

 Do not be fooled by flattery.

When someone gives me hundreds of compliments, I start making the chisel sharper. Do not try to puff me up with flattery. When people do that, they are just trying to hide the real them.

The same people that cried, "Hosanna to the king" were the same to chant, "crucify him!" not long after. The Lord searches our heart not our flattering lips.

If they pump you up enough, you will think that they are really nice and open to receive. However, there is only one time that you will know when someone is really open to receive. That is when you give them their first chisel.

## Looking for Truth

If you correct them and they admit that they have a problem and come to repentance, then they are open to receive. However, you cannot be so quick to believe someone that says, "You are so right."

"No. You are not listening. I said that you have a problem."

"Yes. You are right. I receive, of course."

No, they did not receive. You press until that conviction comes. Until those walls are down, you have not started day one in mentorship.

Let's recap briefly. First you want to build up that trust, get them to talk about themselves, and then, do not go any further until you have seen the real them.

## Things to Look Out For

When the bitterness starts spewing out and there is junk everywhere, then thank the Lord, because you have something to work with. When they say, "I am really nervous and afraid. I do not know what to expect", then praise the Lord.

You are getting a breakthrough. Those are their real feelings. It is not good when you hear, "I had a lot of bitterness, but I have dealt with it now."

"I had that problem once, but the Lord has done such a great work in me."

You should say, "Praise the Lord! What do you need me for then? Bye."

You are there to help people with a problem. If they do not have a problem, then there is nothing for you to do, is there?

They may come to you and say, "I went to the Lord and I prayed about what we discussed last week and He really ministered to me. I have it all together now."

Fantastic! They can just carry on speaking to the Lord then, because you have other people to mentor that actually need your help.

## No Need Needed

It should be about them one hundred percent of the time. If you have a need and they give you a compliment, you will be hurt or affected by it. If you are insecure, the minute they put up a wall, you will be affected by it.

This is why you must focus entirely on them. Read their "halo data". As you continue throughout this book, you will find out what halo data is.

Once you have broken down the walls, you will realize that they have been bitter at their mother since they were born. They hated their father, rejected their sister and kicked their dog. Now you have a starting point.

## Step 2: Meet Their Needs

Now that you know all these things, you have something to work with. It is so easy to see their problems and say, "You are pathetic." No. As their mentor, you need to meet their need for acceptance.

When you have hit them between their eyes and they say, "You know what, I am bitter. I do not even feel like being here." This is when you need to say, "You know what? I understand."

This is when you need to accept them. It is easy to accept someone when they are giving nice compliments, but when you really need to accept someone is when they are demonized, full of oppression, junk, bitterness and they know it.

Give acceptance when it is undeserved.

That is the time to accept them as they are because in that time they cannot see or hear the Lord. They need to have you meet that need first. Then, once you have met that need, you can then move them over to the Holy Spirit, and they can learn to get their need met in the Lord directly.

## Meeting the Need for Acceptance

> *Romans 5:8 But God demonstrates His own love toward us, in that while we were still sinners, Christ died for us.*

Most people do not know how to get that need of acceptance met, so they go from person to person picking up contaminations. If you are a good mentor or trainer, you meet their need for acceptance and recognition so well that they don't go to other people.

If you are working with somebody and they keep going off every five minutes, asking someone else for counsel and their opinion, do not blame them. It is your fault. You did not meet their need. If you did meet their need, then they would not need to go anywhere else. That cuts across a lot of what you may already know.

You must establish a relationship with them first. You have to meet that need. The need for acceptance and recognition is not a sin! It is not a sin to need people or wanting to be recognized.

The sin is having people meet the need, instead of God. Most people do not know how to get that need met in the Lord though, and so that is where you come in. You have to be Christ to them, just like Paul was to the church.

He said, "See Christ in me and be imitators of me." (Phil 3:17) Meet that need and then you can teach them because they will admire you. They will see you as an example, and now you can teach them how to get their needs met in the Lord.

I really want to hammer this point. It is not a sin to have a need for acceptance. It is not a sin to want to be around people. It is not a sin to want to be noticed. It is not sin. It is just being real. God put those needs in us. They are natural.

## Why we Need... Need

If we did not have those needs, we would not get up in the morning. We would not press forward. We would not go from ministry office to ministry office.

It is good to have these needs. In fact, the stronger they are the better because they will propel you forward. The sin is trying to meet that need in others. You should not need any man, but always need and be dependent on God.

I have a co-dependency problem. I am co-dependent on the Holy Spirit. I need Him so badly that I cannot go through a day without Him. That is how it should be. Is that not why Christ came to earth?

## Dealing With the Need

Most people do not understand that. You can say, "You do have that need. It is ok. Let me teach you how to meet it in the Lord." Be Christ to them. Show them His image and what the unconditional love of Jesus is like.

When you come to Jesus with a need for acceptance, does He say, "Deal with it?" No. He does not. He says, "Come. Rest a while with me." If you know the Lord Jesus, you know that He will put His arms around you and say, "I love you unconditionally."

He loves you in all of your sins and all of your failures. The greatest sins are the sins of the heart, not the things that we get wrong every day.

## Identify the Need - Acceptance or Recognition?

The two main needs that drive us all are the needs for acceptance and recognition. Look out for these in your disciple.

Most people do not know that they have these needs, so you have to help them. For some one need is stronger than the other. Look at their relationship with their parents.

 Identify the need – acceptance or recognition?

## What a Need for Acceptance Looks Like

If they had a bad relationship with their mother, then they will have a desperate need for acceptance and they will go around trying to get people to accept and love them.

A mother is meant to accept a child for who they are. If a mother fails, it leaves a gaping need in the life of the child.

They will struggle to build relationships, and they will not have many friends. They will not "know who they are" and will latch on to others to give them a sense of purpose. They will even follow a dominating leader if that person accepts them.

The danger in this is that the enemy is only too happy to send the wrong person along to meet their need. This will lead to a string of bad relationships that are completely need based.

## What a Need for Recognition Looks Like

If they did not have a good relationship with their father, then they do not know where they are going in life. They are running around aimlessly and desiring to be recognized.

The father gives a child a sense of purpose, and helps them rise up into adulthood. A father brings out a son's masculinity and a daughter's femininity.

A father should also help give a child direction for their lives. A mother spends her life building into a child all the materials that they will ever need for success.

Once her job is done, the father takes all those materials and builds a house out of it – giving the child a purpose.

When a father failed, a child will strive their entire life to excel. Inside they are driven to still "prove to dad that they can do it." They will struggle in romantic relationships. Their marriage will be under strain, as they continually push to be a success.

As you meet the need that your disciple has, you will give them acceptance and you will start giving them direction. You can start giving them projects to do and you send them in very specific directions with specific tasks to accomplish.

## Step 3: Minister to Templates of the Past

You are now becoming a surrogate parent to them. As you meet those needs, you start shaping and molding them into the image of Christ. That is where all the templates are going to come up. (Please visit our free article site for more on templates http://www.ami-bookshelf.com )

As you start ministering, sharing and fellowshipping, lots of templates and hurts from the past will come up. I am assuming in this book that you are familiar with our teachings.

If you need to know more about how to deal with templates and hurts from the past, read the bonus chapter *"Templates and Triggers"* at the end of the book because I will not be covering this topic in this chapter.

Templates and triggers will come up. If you have met their need for acceptance and recognition, then they will come to you with their problem and you can minister to the problem and transform the template.

That is true mentorship. It is transforming templates. That is the key, because until our mindsets and our outlook on life have changed, what is within us cannot flow out.

The minute they open their heart to you the impartation of the spiritual things and the gifts, is instant. When you open your heart to someone, you commune spirit to spirit and you receive everything that is in that person's spirit.

You will often pick up the curses your disciples are under. However, if you have dealt with the curses in your life, then they will pick up the blessing and the anointing that you have.

Impartation takes place naturally when hearts are open.

## Do Not Force the Anointing

You do not need to go around chocking people and forcing them to receive your anointing. If both hearts are open, then impartation happens naturally. The problem lies in their templates, their spiritual DNA and the way they view life.

This is what you are there for. When my sister taught me how to make graphics, it was a little easier because I did not know how to do it at all. However, I did have templates on how to put things together and how to take a photograph.

I would put together this really fantastic picture and I would say, "What do you think?" She would say, "You are thinking in a box. You are not applying the principles I taught you. Your thinking is all wrong. Now, let me teach you how to think properly."

It was a different flow. It was not even technical. It was just that I thought in such an analytical and restrictive way that I had to be broken out of it. My sister would say, "Why are you working in such a small space? Make the canvas huge. Play with it. You can always fix it later."

She said, "Be creative and try something crazy." It smashed the way that I thought before. It broke my limited thinking, and just by stepping out in that, I received the spiritual and creative wisdom that God had given her.

I did not need her to lay hands and impart it. I got it by receiving her correction and instruction. The impartation came naturally. That is the work of mentorship, both naturally and spiritually.

You need to work with their templates. Change the way that they think and view things.

## Step 4: Set the Conditions

It is important to set boundaries to your relationship. That way they know what to expect from you and also what you expect from them.

Did you say, "Listen, as your mentor, I expect you to do things my way. I expect you to receive my correction. If you have a problem with it, then you go and pray, receive the correction and then come back to me. If that is not acceptable for you, then I do not want to be your mentor."

You are too afraid to do that, aren't you? If you do that, then that means that they will reject you and they will not want to be your disciple. If that is the case, then thank the Lord because you do not want a disciple like that.

You set the terms and the conditions. You tell them what you expect because what you have is very valuable. Your time is very valuable and they can thank the Lord that you are even taking the time to chat with them and give them this opportunity.

Mentoring is not your only ministry. You have many other things to do and you are taking time out of what you usually would be doing to impart to them, so that they can rise up and be like you.

They better know that you are giving them gold. If a CEO comes to a new employee and offers to spend time with him and to put everything on hold for him, does the employee say, "Thanks for the invitation, but I am busy, so I will get back to you when it is convenient for me?"

No way! He knows that the CEO has so many other things he could be doing or places that he could be, but instead he is spending time specifically with him. If we have this understanding in the natural world, then why not in the spiritual also?

I am an apostle. I stand in a ministry office. You should appreciate that I am giving you an opportunity to rise up, because I could be spending this time with somebody else, writing another book, putting out another message or going to a conference.

However, I am spending time with you instead. You better know that my time is valuable. Does that sound arrogant? Good. It better be arrogant because they are not going to admire you if you do not know "who" you are, and if you do not appreciate what God has put in you.

Do you realize that your skill is just that? It is a skill and a talent. Try going to a bible school or anywhere in this world and learn from them.

"Do you realize what treasure I am giving you right now? If you do not like it, go away!"

I cannot tell you how many times I have had to say that to people. My time is too valuable to sit and argue with people about whether I am right or wrong. It is one thing if you are a pastor of a church. It is another if you are mentoring someone.

Did Jesus ask for anything less? His disciples paid a hefty price to follow Him and to receive his anointing. Not everyone could pay that price and not everyone was necessarily called to.

However, if your disciple wants what you have, then they should be prepared to pay the same price that you paid to get it!

"If you do not want to receive what I say, then please move! Somebody else is waiting for your seat."

Do you have that arrogance? Are you as arrogant as Paul? Can you say, "Imitate me. Do as I do. Will I have to come with a rod or not?" (1 Cor 4:21)

How many Timothys were there? There was only one Timothy and one Titus. I am sure that there were many that would have liked to receive what Timothy had received. Yet, it is Timothy that is in the Scriptures right now.

He had all that wealth of knowledge, experience, ability and anointing that Paul had, and so do we. They say that salvation is free. Yes, it is free for us, but for Christ it cost Him everything.

## Salvation Came With a High Price

These gifts, offices and spiritual abilities that we have, we received by paying a price. We received these things through travail, death, blood, sweat and tears. I received these things from the Lord at a high price.

If I am going to spend time with you, then I better know that you are willing to pay the price. I will not waste my time on someone that is not prepared to pay the price. When I call a disciple, I want to know, "Are you a Timothy or not?"

"Are you going to follow through or not?"

It is up to you to set the conditions. Yet, the problem is in your mind again. It is good that you have come to the place of realizing that you have nothing.

You and I both know that when you go through ministry training, you come to a place of realizing that you are weak and foolish. You know that if it were not for Christ, you would be nothing, but an empty, clanging bell.

It is good that you know that, but there is treasure in earthen vessels. You may just be an earthen vessel, but there is a treasure within you. Do not look down your nose at that treasure. God went to the extreme of coming to this earth and hanging around with unfaithful, rotten humans.

Then on top of all that, He died on the cross for them. He did this to put that treasure inside of you. He paid a great price to give us this inheritance. So do not look down at it as if it were nothing, because it is everything.

Realize what you have and that there are people out there that need it. If they are not going to take it seriously, then push them aside and get someone else that does want to take it seriously.

What you have is important and if they do not think so, then you do not want to work with them. Am I starting to give you a picture of who you are in Christ, and who you are in the body of Christ? Until you have that picture, you have nothing to impart.

# CHAPTER 06:
# Mentorship: Do's & Don'ts

*Matthew 10:16 Behold, I send you out as sheep in the midst of wolves. Therefore be wise as serpents and harmless as doves.*

Disciples will eat you alive. They will gnaw at your ankles and eat you a piece at a time, until they have sucked the life out of you, unless you know what you are doing. (Ok, so I am known to be a tad dramatic. Just roll with it!)

That is why you have to be as wise as a serpent, but as harmless as a dove.

Have your wits about you. On the other hand though, do not be afraid to be loving and tender to give acceptance. It is a tough world. People are selfish. They will take what they can and spit you out, unless you change that mentality in them.

## Prepare for the Worst. Hope for the Best

Mentorship is about changing their mentality. Prepare for failure. If you go with that mentality and then they are a success, then it is wonderful. However, do not just expect them to understand from the beginning.

They do not know how to be a disciple. That is why you are mentoring them. You assume that since you are mentoring them, that they already know how to be a disciple. They do not know, and this is why you must lay it out for them and give them a clear track to run on.

> No one is born knowing how to be a disciple.

This is why I said that mentorship is a skill that you can learn. You do not just hop into a relationship and say, "Let's wing it and see what happens as we go." You will end up running around in circles and never arrive anywhere.

You will not know when the mentorship started, ended or why you are in it. You will think, "Why did I even bother?" It is your fault... not theirs.

Here you are thinking, "This disciple is so rebellious. They did not even receive my correction." Well, did you tell them that they had to?

## What Not to Do

## 1. No Uncertainty

Do not show shock or uncertainty. You must have it together. You are going to hear some wild stories. They are going to share their life story with you and you are going to think, "Wow. I thought I had it bad."

When those moments come, do not be moved, surprised or shocked. You have heard it all. They need you to not be shocked or surprised. They need you to have it together and to have all the answers. That is why they came to you.

One time, one of my children came to me after she had fallen and there was blood everywhere. I started screaming frantically, "Oh my goodness, there is blood! There is blood!"

My husband, Craig, had to come and calm both me, and the child down. Who do you think the child is going to go to next time they are bleeding? It is definitely not going to be Mommy.

When you are in a panic, you do not need everyone around you to panic too. When someone comes to you and they are cut and bleeding and there is a whole spiritual hemorrhage going on, you should not get hysterical.

You need to say, "Ok. It is just a cut. Come to the bathroom and let's put some antiseptic on it and you will be just fine. We will get you some stitches and everything will be alright."

Feel free to die on the inside, but on the outside you must have things under control. They need you to be like that. If you stay calm, then so will they. Then they will open their heart and share.

However, if you say, "Never in my life have I heard anything like that." Then they are not going to ask you for counsel. Maybe you will need to get on the phone with someone later and ask for help on how to deal with what they shared, but for now you understand and you do not show shock.

## 2. Watch out for Condemnation

Second, do not ever allow yourself to come under condemnation. You might say to someone that they have a need for acceptance. In response they say to you, "No, I actually had a good relationship with my mother and I do not feel like I need people at all?"

What are you going to do then? Are you going to say, "Oh, sorry I must have misinterpreted or missed it?" No. You are not going to apologize. You are going to say, "That could be so, but this is what I sense and see. If I see it from this side, then there is a problem."

Do not come under condemnation. There will be times when you will make a wrong judgment but that is fine. The Lord will use it. It does not matter whether you are right or wrong.

One time I walked in the lounge and saw shoes on the floor and I said to my daughter, "Jessica, How many times have I told you not to leave your shoes on the floor?"

"But Mommy... "

"I do not want to hear it. Put your shoes away!"

"But Mommy... "

Then Deborah came in and said, "Ruby put Jessica's shoes on the floor."

Oh boy. Now I had punished her but it was not even her fault and I felt so bad about it. However, she should not have done the "but Mommy" thing.

If she would have walked up to me and said, "Yes Mom, I will put them upstairs," she would not have gotten in trouble. Sure, I was in the wrong, but there was still a better way for her to respond.

The Lord will use every situation for their learning. He will even use your mistakes. They should know how to respond to that. If they can respond to you correctly, then they will be able to respond to others in the world correctly.

### Life is Not Fair

This is the reality. Life is not fair. If they can learn to handle that unfairness with you, then they can learn to handle it with others. Do not ever come under condemnation or try to defend yourself.

## 3. Never Act Under Pressure

Do not ever feel under pressure from your disciple or anyone else. You do not have to feel like, "They wrote to me and I have to answer now." No. The Holy Spirit never pushes.

I do not care if they phoned you five times this week. You do not have to meet them. You do not have to do anything. God is never moved by need. He is moved by faith.

Until they come to a place where they are ready to receive, you do not offer them anything. If you charge in under pressure, you are neither helping yourself nor them. You are going to come away drained, discouraged and frustrated.

Do not ever respond under pressure. I do not care if you have not spoken to them in three months or even if they are at going through family drama. Until God says move, you do not move! It is very simple. You do not move under pressure.

The Holy Spirit is the only one that is allowed to put pressure on you. Do not ever allow yourself to come under that condemnation or pressure. You stay on top and you stay in control. If you fail, the Lord will sort you out later.

Yet, remember that even if you fail, the Lord will use your failures.

## What to Do

## 1. Share Appropriate Stories Only

Only share stories to illustrate, not to meet your own needs. Do not think, "Finally! Somebody that has to listen to me," and then proceed to telling them your life story. They do not care. They do not want to or need to hear your story.

The less they know about you, the better. The only time you share your story, is when you are illustrating a point. If I am ministering to someone that is pregnant, I will say, "I know how that feels. It is perfectly normal. Every pregnant woman goes through that. Relax."

You do not need to tell the whole story. Yet, sometimes it helps to share a bit so that it makes you seem more human. Sometimes it is good for them to know that they are not the only person going through that specific issue.

If they really admire you and know that you have been through the same thing, it is sometimes very reassuring to them. You may have a disciple that says, "I really have a problem with lust."

It may be ok for you to say, "There was a time in my life when I had a problem with that, and this is the solution. Also, know that God does not condemn you." It is ok to share a story when it is necessary and it helps them in their situation.

This is especially helpful with sensitive subjects that people are embarrassed to talk about. A woman may come to you and say, "There is a problem in me and my husband's sexual relationship. I do not feel like having sex very often."

If you are a woman, you can say, "Sometimes that happens to me as well, but it is ok… and this is how you deal with that." You may even find out that there is another problem. What you are doing with your illustration is taking the spotlight off them and putting it on yourself. By doing that, it relaxes them and they realize that they are normal.

## 2. Take the Spotlight off Sensitive Subjects

When a subject is very sensitive it is important that you take the spotlight off of them. If you have a couple that cannot control their kids, then you can share a story of your own.

I would say, "When my children were younger, I really battled to keep them under control. They would pull the place to pieces and everyone would get mad. One day I journaled about it and the Lord told me the most profound thing!

After I applied what God told me, I found out that they can be obedient, as long as I set the right boundaries." Then they will open up and say, "Really? My oldest always does that." Then you can say, "I know just what you mean. Do 'this' and 'that'."

Their heart will be wide open and they will know that you know what you are talking about. Otherwise, they will say, "What do you know? You do not even have kids." Only share personal stories when they are going to help them in their situation.

They do not need to know more than that. They only need to know the part that applies to them. Again, you only need to use that to take the pressure off of them, so that they will come out of their shells a bit.

## 3. Speak Only When Led

Speak only when led, and only answer when you feel the go ahead in the spirit. Do not be pressured to say anything. If you do not get revelation, reassure them, but do not feel like you need to give counsel.

Sometimes people just need to talk. Do not just be quiet and say nothing. Just know that it is ok to not give counsel all the time. Sometimes people will share their entire life story and all that is necessary is for you to say, "I understand. Man... that must have been tough. How did you handle that? How did that make you feel?"

Do not feel like you have to tell them what their problem is, and be pushed to counsel all of the time. Let the Holy Spirit minister through you. You are just the vessel. Relax. Keep your composure. Do not get flustered, especially if you do not know the answer.

There is nothing worse than someone coming to you for ministry and they say, "This is my problem." Then, you sit there and pray, and get nothing. So you start thinking that you missed the Lord, and you start to feel insecure.

No. Stop right there. You tell them that the Lord is not giving you any revelation right now, because whatever they are going through they do not have a full understanding of yet and they just need to wait a while.

Tell them that there is more that the Holy Spirit wants to show them, and that you do not want to rush into anything. You can arrange to get together for lunch next week and then talk about it again later.

There have been many times when people have come to me with their problems or even after I had chiseled them and they asked, "Can we pray now?" I tell them, "No. We cannot pray now. I am sorry. I do not have a magic wand for you to make all your problems go away. Unless the Lord talks, I am not talking. So no, we are not ready to pray now. You have not even gotten a conviction yet."

I will often tell people that we will not pray yet, and that I will decide when we will pray and when we won't pray. I tell them that they cannot not just come and ask me to pray at their command. I will pray when the Holy Spirit tells me to.

 Pray when the Holy Spirit tells you to pray.

A good counselor is not moved by demands – he is moved by the Holy Spirit. So do not come under condemnation.

The Scriptures say that the Holy Spirit manifests the gifts as He wills. (1 Cor 12:11) If you are not getting any revelation, then He is not manifesting the gifts right now. You are not a psychic. Do not try to be one.

If He is not giving revelation, then they do not have faith or the Lord is not ready to talk. "Sorry. The Lord is not talking. Come back another day."

It keeps you in control and it reassures them that you know what to do in the situation.

There is nothing worse than babbling and saying all the wrong things. That will only make them feel more insecure. All you need to do is say that you do not think it is time to pray or talk about that thing yet.

You can let them know that you do not feel led, and that you feel that they are getting into something that they do not need to be digging around in right now.

Often, soon after that, the Lord will give the answer and then you can go back to them and resolve the issue in His time.

## 4. Think From Their Perspective

Always love and think from their perspective. Often you can forget what it is like and how it feels to be where they are.

They are facing rejection and then you say, "The problem is that you are too insecure. You need to deal with this rejection template, and rise up."

Do you remember what it was like back there? Do you remember what it felt like to feel that rejection and how uncontrollable the emotions were?

Sure, now it is all over and you have dealt with it, but they have not dealt with it yet. You cannot just brush it off, ask them to have it together and feel good. It is not going to happen.

You need to understand things from their perspective. Try to remember what it was like when you were at the level they are at now. Do you remember what you thought and felt? That is how they are feeling right now.

Do not over-identify, but understand where they are at, and then lead them into the new thing. Realize that they need your help. That is why you are there with them.

## 5. Expect Obedience

Parents expect respect and obedience from their children. You should expect the same from your intern or disciple. I am going to say this again - do not be so humble and just wait for them to give you a call whenever they can or whenever they feel like it.

Also when you correct them, you should expect them to obey. If I say to a child, "Do not put your hand in the fire." I do not say it halfheartedly. I am being serious. I mean "do not do it" and I expect them to obey.

In the same way, you should expect that obedience from your disciple. If they do not obey, you say, "I am disappointed. Why did you not obey when I gave you a direct project?

That was out of line and it is unacceptable to me. If we are going to work together, then you will need to do what I have told you to do. If I tell you to read this book, then read this book. If I tell you to do a project and get back to me next week, then do the project and get back to me by next week."

When you expect that, it will give them security. Perhaps you think that you are being a dominating and horrible leader, but you are not. You are bringing them security. If you did not give them those guidelines, they would do whatever they want.

They will feel insecure and you will not know what is going on with them. Then you are going to get frustrated with them and say that they will never amount to anything. Well, did you give them the guidelines? Did you let them know what was expected of them?

Do not be afraid to set your standards. They will receive through respect. Then when you give instructions, they will take them seriously. Also, show your respect, fear and admiration for those that are over you.

## 6. Lift Your Leaders Up

Do not be too afraid or insecure to lift up leaders that you admire, because they will follow your example. When you are insecure, you will think that when those you train rise up higher than you, will no longer admire you.

That is not true at all. When I am at home and I say to my daughters, "Your dad is the best and he is the boss of this home." Do they stop loving me? No. That gives them a good image to imitate.

Do you lift up your mentor? Do you continually extol the virtues of your spiritual parents? Do you say that you want to be just like them? Are you giving your disciples that image?

When you lift up others, they will in turn admire you. However, if you are insecure and you put yourself at the top and say you are the best all the time, then what image are you giving your disciples?

When the mentorship is over, they will end up treating you the same way you treated your leaders. If you do not give respect and admiration to those that respect and admiration is due, know that you will reap what you sow.

### Applies to Peers Also

I am not saying this to only those that are above you, but even to your peers. Are you afraid to lift up those around you higher than yourself? Are you willing to make them look really good and put yourself under them?

If you can do that, then you will give your disciple an image to follow. If you want to bring unity to the body of Christ, then unite yourself with others and give an example and image of unity.

### Living by Your Own Rules

It is not enough to speak about it. You have to be that image. Are you as a mentor fulfilling all of the proper roles that I have discussed as a disciple and a spiritual child? Are you obedient? Do you submit? Are you following the guidelines?

Are you doing all of the things that you are expecting your disciple to do? If you are not, then I have bad news for you. You have a bad time ahead of you, because your disciples are going to treat you just like you have treated others.

When they rise up with your skill and come alongside you, they are going to push you down and raise themselves up just like you did. They are going to pretend that there is nobody else in the world with their skill - just like you did.

That is why you need to deal with your own needs and insecurities and have them met first. This is so important. Lift up those that you admire. Do not be afraid to say that you really admire someone.

Do be not afraid to say, "Do you see who I am? I am this because of what my spiritual parents poured into me!" Do you think saying that makes me less of an apostle? No. It makes you think, "I want that attitude too."

Jesus did it too. The Scriptures say that although Jesus was equal to God and higher than the angels, He set Himself under them. He came to the earth. He was as high as God and He humbled Himself. (Phil 2:7)

He would constantly refer to the Father and say, "I do what I see my Father do." He consistently lifted up His

Father in the sight of the people. When the disciples' turn came, what did they do?

They lifted Jesus up just like Jesus did with His Father. If you want to bring unity and the correct pattern, then you need to live it. Live it in not only what you say, but in what you do.

 You will change as much as they will.

You are God's vessel in His hands. You are His chisel and His oil. He will fill you up and pour you out. As you are working on shaping the vessel that God has given you, the hand of God is going to come upon you, shape you and change you too.

Your insecurities will have no choice but to go. The Lord will deal with everything that hinders your ability as a mentor. There is nothing like having the anointing of God flow through you as you are working on someone else.

## The Potter's Wheel

It is like the potter's wheel. You may just be the wheel, but you are going to get splattered with clay and you will get changed along with the vessel. You will change as much as them.

With each mentorship experience you have, you will gain more experience and learn more about life. Do not think that you have all the answers from the start and that you are just going to get in there and change the world.

Yes, you will change the world, but you will go through some changes along the way yourself. You are going to make some mistakes too. It is like having a child for the first time. When you look back on your first-born, you think of all the mistakes you made.

However, by time the third or fourth child comes along, you will do the job with your eyes closed. You will have that baby bathed, dressed and put to sleep in fifteen minutes.

You learn as you go and you never arrive. That is what I love about the realm of the spirit and about being an apostle. You never get there. There is always another horizon or adventure.

 **Tools of the Trade**

## Knowing Your Intern

Every person brings a new joy into your life. This is a good experience. I have a worksheet below called *Knowing Your Intern*. It is a trainer worksheet for you to apply to your ministry right now.

Let's start by going through these questions quickly and see if you can answer them.

### Know Yourself

1.  Think of someone that you are mentoring or someone that looks up to you. (Those that look up to you are the ones that you usually end up mentoring and pouring out all that you have to. Those are the ones that you need to start with.)

    Write down those names because you will need them for the rest of the questions.

2.  Your Abilities

    a.  What are your personal abilities?

    b.  What are your spiritual and natural gifts?

        Make a note of them. Then with that in mind, answer the following:

    c.  What is it that you are mentoring each person in from the list in question 1?

This will set the tone for the whole mentorship relationship.

### Know Your Intern

From the list of names above, answer the following questions regarding each intern.

1.  What is their temperament?

2.  What kind of relationship did they have with their parents?

    Once you know that, you will see where their hang-ups, needs, issues and templates are.

3.  Do they have a stronger need for acceptance or recognition? (Or Both?)

    Yes, they will naturally have that need, but assess which is stronger or if they are both just as strong?

4.  What are their ministry desires?

    If you do not know how to find this out, then get our *The Fivefold Ministry* series.

5.  What wrong mindsets do they have in the area that you are mentoring them in?

    If you are mentoring someone in graphics and they do not know how to switch on a computer, then you need to make a note of that. Note all obvious areas that they need help in.

This will give you a track to run on, so that whenever the Holy Spirit brings these things up, you are prepared on how to deal with it.

As time goes on you will not need these instructions anymore because they will be in you. I am mentoring you right now in this book, am I not?

6.  **What is their level of transparency and willingness to change?**

    Until they are transparent with you and willing to change, you cannot start intense mentorship. You need to assess that at the beginning.

7.  **What is the condition of their personal relationships?**

    You want to know if they are married, who they are married to, why they are married and what the relationship is like?

    If you are mentoring one spouse and their relationship is bad, then you have one serious problem on your hands. The Word says that the two shall become one flesh, so if you are touching one, then you are touching the other.

    The condition of their marriage is extremely important. You will often spend the majority of your time giving marital counsel and telling them what to do with their spouse or family.

If they are single, do they ever want to get married? If not, that is a big red flag. That shows that there are some issues. There are more than likely insecurities, fear of commitment, fear of failure and many other fears.

8. Make note of the kind of relationships that they have - especially the intimate ones.

   For example, if they are living at home with their parents, what kind of relationship do they have with their parents?

Their relationships are going to affect your mentorship relationship, so be prepared ahead of time.

I have covered a lot of ground, so you will want to go over this chapter a few times. However, I will repeat some things throughout the book. Plus, what I want you to pick up the most is the spirit and the wisdom of what I am teaching.

Realize that you are a vessel in the hands of God. When you know who you are, then passing on what you have will be so much easier. I can give you the what to do and what not to do, but at the end of the day it is up to you to take this treasure that God has given you and to impart it to others.

Know what that treasure is. Be willing to be that vessel and the rest will flow out naturally.

# CHAPTER 07:
# Phase 1 – The Mentorship Structure

*2 Kings 2:15 Now when the sons of the prophets who were from Jericho saw him, they said, "The spirit of Elijah rests on Elisha." And they came to meet him, and bowed to the ground before him.*

Can you remember your school days? Most of us would probably rather forget them. If we think back on our childhood though, the first thing that comes to mind is our school days. You especially think of the things you hated most about them.

The thing I hated the most about school was not the teachers or the work, but having to get up so early in the morning. I loved to sleep in. On Saturdays and Sundays I would sleep the whole day away.

I did not like getting up at the crack of dawn. I had to get ready in 15 minutes, quickly grab something to eat and then dive into traffic so I could board the school bus on time. To top that off, the teacher was standing up front trying to pump all their knowledge into my head.

## The Bad Old Days

At that time, I did not even have my morning cup of coffee yet. It was horrible. The structure was awful. Everything about it was so difficult. Yet, that was the place of learning and that is what took me through a lot of experiences in life that formed me into the person I am now.

Whether we like it or not, as humans, we need that structure in our lives to help give us a direction and to shape us. We would have never been in a position to learn any subject, if we did not have a structure to learn it in.

I sat in math class and learned from my teacher because we had time schedules set up. We had days where we had to go to math class. We had a structure and because of that structure, the classes could flow one after the other very simply.

This made it possible to receive from teacher after teacher. If I had to talk about the educational system and what I thought about that, I would take a whole different turn in this book, so I am not going to get into the education side.

## Setting up the Structure

However, I am going to speak about the structure. Even in the Scriptures, Paul speaks about having instructors. He said that we have many instructors, but few spiritual fathers. (1 Cor 4:15)

There is nothing wrong with having or being an instructor. Is that not what mentorship is? A mentor is an instructor. Just like you had a certain time you needed to be in class by, and a certain subject that you had to learn at specific levels, so will you need to set a structure when mentoring someone as well.

They need to know their boundaries and you need to know yours because within that structure, you can teach and they can learn. Could you imagine everyone coming to school whenever they felt like it?

What if some slept in until ten in the morning, someone else slept in until noon and so everyone just wandered into math class whenever they wanted to.

Imagine the teacher sitting around waiting for everyone to arrive.  The only once everyone arrived would she start to scramble around and decide what to teach.

Imagine her looking at her book saying, "What should I teach you today? Calculus? Trig? Let's just look at some Geometry."

How much would anyone learn with that lack of structure? Children think that it would be so cool to get up and learn whenever they wanted to.

The truth is that they would not really learn much at all. When it comes to learning and instruction, there need to be boundaries and rules. As humans, we feel comfortable within those rules.

 Everyone needs structure for successful learning.

This relates to every area of your life, whether you are at home or at work, there will come a time when you need to receive or give instruction.

## Mentorship, a Step at a Time

In the first few chapters, I gave you a very clear overview of what mentorship is about. You saw who you should be as a mentor and what you should be offering as a mentor. Now I want to start breaking that message down and look at things practically step by step.

I am going to give you instructions based on high level mentorship. You can use it for lower level mentorship as well, but it is primarily going to be about fivefold ministry, and leadership mentorship.

I will often be talking about the kind of mentorship relationship in which you are raising up ministers, leaders and people to become successful in life.

## Step 1. Initiate Mentorship

So you have a disciple that has been released into some form of ministry training and you feel that the Lord is calling you to mentor this person. How do you know when somebody is ready to receive from you as a mentor?

You do not know because you do not wait around for someone to decide whether they want you to be their mentor or not. You will not know until you ask them.

You can receive a prompting by the Holy Spirit, feel an impression in your spirit or simply out of pure love, decide to devote your time to them because you know that you have something that they need.

How will you know when they are ready? You will only know when you ask them!

 How will you know if someone is ready? When you ask them!

You have to approach the disciple. That is what Elijah did with Elisha. He threw his mantle on him. (1 Kings 19:19)

## The Mentor Always Calls the Disciple

Samuel chose King David, and King David chose Solomon. The one who has the authority needs to call the disciple. The mentor always calls the disciple. You will not know if that person is ready to receive, until you call them to mentorship.

There is a lot of confusion between mentorship and spiritual fatherhood.

## Do Not Confuse Mentorship and Spiritual Parenting

Keep in mind that mentorship is a temporary relationship. Secondly, the mentor chooses the disciple. With spiritual parenting it is the other way around. The relationship in a spiritual parenting relationship is permanent and the child chooses the parent.

It is only in a parenting relationship that the child chooses who they are going to admire and look up to. If you mix these two, you will go around in circles and you will never take that person to the level of maturity that you should. You will be shooting in the dark.

It will be like us going to school whenever we feel like it and just hanging around until the teacher feels like teaching. What happens when this takes place? You learn nothing and get nowhere.

You need a structure and a track to run on when you are mentoring someone. Firstly, you must call them. Secondly, you must make them aware of what is to be expected on this journey.

## Step 2. Define the Mentorship Relationship

If I invite someone to come around for dinner, they have a picture in their mind of what to expect when they come over. They may ask, "Should I bring anything with me?"

Then I can say, "Do not worry about it. I have taken care of it. We will be going 'here'. We will be doing this'." I make it clear. You do not just spring a meal on someone. They should know what to expect.

It is the same in school. You know what to expect. In South Africa, where I am from, on your first day of school you attend the orientation. They take you around the whole school and show you the different classrooms, tell you what time you have to be at school, how many classes you will have and you may even meet some teachers.

This way, before you officially begin school, you already know what to expect. How many times do you spring mentorship on someone and they do not even have a clue about what to expect?

Half way down the line you get annoyed with them because they are not doing what you expect them to do, but you never told them what you expected in the first place.

Mentorship is not a "hit and miss" thing. You cannot just feel the direction of the wind and "see how it goes". You must not only choose the direction of the wind but also define how hard it is going to blow. You must decide where they are going to go and how they are going to get there.

In mentorship you have to give a structure to your disciple. You set their pace and their direction. You give them the tests. To do that you need to have foresight.

## Have a Plan Ahead of Time

You should have decided ahead of time, the expectations that you have for this disciple, the expectations God has for this disciple and which track you are going to set them on.

Can you see the responsibility that you have as a mentor?

It is not just something that you hope comes right. This is something that you have to prepare for and be very sure about. So, let me give you step one again.

Call your disciple. Say, "I am calling you to this specific training." Do not say, "Come and be my disciple." A disciple of what exactly? I mentioned this in the previous chapters. You cannot just say to them, "You are my disciple. Hang around me, wash my hands, clean my car and just be there and think I am a cool guy." That is not mentorship.

What are you mentoring them into? Be clear. "I am mentoring you into apostolic office."

"I am mentoring you into pastoral office."

"I am mentoring you into entrepreneurship"

"I am mentoring you into motherhood"

"I am mentoring you into becoming a good wife/husband."

Be very specific.

## Step 3. Share Your Expectations

Now, after you have chosen what you are going to mentor them into, explain to them what they are getting into. It will sound something like this:

"During the phase of mentorship, if you accept my offer, I will expect obedience and submission. I expect you to read what I tell you to read. I want you to know that I am going to test and challenge you.

I am going to give you direction. I do not want you stepping out without coming to me first. I do not want you going off, prophesying and doing your own thing without coming to me first, so that I can give you instruction.

I want one hundred percent communication from you. I want you to write to me twice a day."

If that is what you want, make it clear. Do not just hope that they will know. They do not know. That is why they are the disciples.

They are like me when I was a little six-year-old that had never been to school before. I did not know what school buildings looked like and I had never been in one. How was I supposed to know there were classes every day and that I had to travel from class to class?

## Boundaries are Essential

How was I supposed to know that classes began at a certain time each day? I did not have a clue. I had to be taught those things. I had to be given my boundaries. Then when I stepped out of line, I was disciplined.

However, you cannot go around getting annoyed when your disciple is not doing what you want them to do when you have not given them their boundaries. You cannot tell them they are wrong about something, when you have never laid down the law and given them a structure in the first place.

## Step 4. Send Them to Teachings

Give very clear instructions on what to do next. If someone is released into prophetic training and you feel like you are the one to mentor them, then you need to do what it takes to get them into office. By the way, if you are the one that releases them into training, then you are automatically obligated to carry them through to office in some type of way.

If you have a course of materials (like we do in our ministry), you are blessed. You do not have to run around hysterically trying to figure out what you are going to teach them and how you are going to train them.

You can pick up *The Prophet's Field Guide* series and say, "Here are twenty six lessons of power-packed death and resurrection that will take any prophet from ministry to office in nine months flat."

It does not get any easier than that. That is the next direction that you want to give anybody who has come to mentorship. Let them know what you are raising them up into and give them the expectations and instructions.

Then tell them to make their choice and let them know that you are not going to sit around waiting. Elisha said to Elijah, "I need to go bury my folks and then I can come with you and carry on with my calling."

Elijah pretty much said, "Do not waste my time. I am out of here." Be specific. You can say, "This is a one-time offer. You accept it now or do not accept it at all. I have other people that want me to work with them."

Once they accept the offer and say, "I commit to you and submit to you as my mentor and I am on this road," then the training really begins.

So the first thing that you want to do is get them into some good teaching.

The anointing in the teachings and the Word itself will act as a double-edged sword that will separate the joint and the marrow, the soul and the spirit. Do not feel that you have to shape them in your own strength.

## You do Not Wield Yourself

This is a big mistake that mentors often make. Sure, you are God's tool to shape and change them. Yet, remember that you are GOD'S tool, not your own tool. You do not wield yourself. God wields you. Never forget that.

Do not decide that you must make them into a prophet now and think about what you did and do it to them and see what happens. That is not how it works. The Holy Spirit will bring the chisel and the challenges.

 Once the mentorship relationship is established, get them into teachings.

As a mentor, it is for you to guide, direct and make them aware of what the Holy Spirit is already doing in their life. The problem is though if they are not on the path, you cannot guide, direct or make them aware, can you?

That is why the first thing you have to do is get them into the Word and the teachings. Your first project every time, without fail, will be to lead them to do a certain project, course, read a book or watch a certain message.

In my personal opinion, if you have it available for them, I tell them to watch or listen to the teachings because I want them to pick up the anointing. When you watch and listen to a lecture, you receive it easier.

If there is a language barrier or you only have reading materials, then that is fine too. Giving them the materials and the track makes them feel secure and it gives you something to start with.

You can also take a bit of a break while they are chowing and choking on those materials and dying a bit. They will think that you are the greatest mentor in the world and you can have the time to sit and get all the other work done that you have.

## Step 5. Make Instructions Specific

After you have given them a track to run on and told them what to do, very clearly explain to them what you want them to do with that information. Do not simply say, "Go and read this book." You and I are already in office, so it is obvious to us what has to be done.

However, it is not obvious for others who are coming down the road for the first time. I remember on my first day of school, I needed to go to the bathroom. I held it for as long as I could because the thought of leaving the classroom was terrifying.

### The Bad Bathroom Experience

Yet, I could not hold it. I had to go. Eventually, I put my hand up and asked the teacher to go to the bathroom and so I walked out. Then on the way back to the classroom from the bathroom, I did not recognize anything.

If anyone knows me, they know that my bad sense of direction has been there since I was a child. I stepped out of the bathroom and I did not know where I was. I did not know where to go.

Then I saw a classroom that looked like mine. I went racing into it and when I got inside, it was packed with a room full of seniors. I was mortified. I burst into the classroom and everyone stopped what they were doing and just stared at me.

Then one of the seniors that were in the class took me by the hand and guided me into my correct classroom. Yes, a few years down the line, I then knew where everything was, but I was new at everything at first and I did not have a clue.

It was obvious to the seniors because they had been in school for a while, but it was not obvious to me. Do not think it is obvious for your disciple, what to think, do and read.

 Assume nothing. Until you give instruction, your disciple will not know what to do.

They do not know. That is why they are with you. They need mentorship. You have to think for them and think ahead. They do not think like you yet. They do not even think like the Lord yet.

They do not even know how to prophesy or study properly. Take them through it a step at a time. Tell them what to read and to report back at a specific time and tell them what you expect to be in the report.

## The Instruction I Give My Disciples

I personally give my disciples a list of things that I would like them to listen to or read. Then I tell them to give me a report on:

1. What they felt when they listened?

2. What convictions God gave them when they listened?

3. What thoughts came to their mind during the teaching?

By doing that, if they feel something, I can identify if there are any templates that were addressed, what God convicted them on, where they are in their training and what they thought about and really learned.

Those three very simple questions give me a clear indication of where they are at in their training right now and what needs to be worked on. When they give me that report, I can then give them a practical project.

If they come back to me and say, "I was really challenged when he spoke about pouring out one hundred percent and having an other-orientation. I panicked a bit and felt that I could not do that.

I am not secure in this area. I really felt convicted when he spoke about God telling you to stand out in your weakness. I knew God was calling me to do that."

## I Give a Project

As a mentor, you have the first project to give them.

Using the example above, I would give that disciple one of my "other-orientation" projects. It is that simple.

You can clearly identify the area that God is working on in them and they even got the revelation for themselves. You do not have to dig it up from somewhere.

By doing this you will learn to draw out of their spirit what God has put in there. You do not need to tell them to do projects and learning against their will. The Holy Spirit will use you as a vessel to draw them, teach them and shape them.

## Continual Feedback Essential

You are an active part in this. Continually get feedback from them. Do not just try to wing it or simply dwell on revelation. You must communicate. What did you feel? What did you sense? What did you think?

When they give you answers, it will be obvious what to do. You may even feel that they are getting into deception. Some of the things that they share with you may sound way off and out of line with the Word of God.

If someone like that is in prophetic training, you can let them know that they are living the prophetic deception portion of their training and lead them to the *Prophetic Counter Insurgence* book.

Often you will feel that before they move onto the next lesson, they should listen to something about hurts from the past or about dealing with curses.

## Dealing with Hurts from the Past

There are times when you may find that you are throwing them into many different directions. Sometimes when some of my interns listened to *Signs of the Prophetic Calling*, all the hurts of their past suddenly came up. They realized how many bad experiences they had with their parents and all the rejection they faced.

 Sometimes in ministry mentorship, you will need to break from regular teachings and minister to hurts.

When this happens, I send them to a message on hurts, bitterness and anger. If you are mentoring someone into a ministry office and hurts from the past suddenly come up, do not even go another step forward with the regular ministry teachings.

Take a break and minister to the hurts, otherwise they will not be fit enough to handle the intensity of the training further down the road.

That is why you need to have that feedback. Then once they have done what you said, get them back on track with their original course.

## The Use of Practical Projects

Each time they dig into the Word or the teachings, the Holy Spirit will use it to bring things up in them. When this happens give them projects to do. The projects must be practical. Make sure that after everything you have them do, that they continue to report back to you.

If they have a problem with other-orientation, tell them that you want them to do something good for every one of their co-workers that week. Tell them to make a list of people in their church and give them an encouraging word or do something out of love for them.

Then have them report back to you. Teach them to communicate. See how it goes. They may come back and say, "I failed. It was tough." Then you can say, "It is because you have a template here and these things are standing in the way."

You cannot address things like that if you do not get any feedback. Also, you cannot address anything if they do not have the Word in them. You are not the standard. The Word of God is the standard.

No teacher at school stands up and says, "This is what I think about algebra." They pick up the textbook and they say, "This is the way it is. These are the facts. This is the science of it."

 Mentorship is a science. Stick to the facts.

Mentorship is also a science. The science is that the Word of God says this, this and that. Do not go by what you feel or what you think they should be. Go by the Word of God.

### The Disciple Will Not Doubt the Word

If you use our teachings to help you mentor, then you have an additional blessing. Refer back to them again and again. Your disciple may doubt you from time to time, but they will not doubt the materials or the Word of God as quickly.

Use that as your authority. Do not stand in your own authority. Use the materials and the Word of God as your authority. If all else fails, use the leader above you as your authority. Just do not stand in your own authority. Remember, you are a tool and a vessel.

## Tools of the Trade

Take note of this. Remember that no matter what they go through or experience during the time of their training, you must take all of those things and point them back to their training.

I have a couple of lessons that I use with my interns. They are general ones. Getting involved, other-orientation, communication projects and things like that. (Available in The Mentor's Book of Projects)

I can take each one of those subjects and apply them differently according to what I am mentoring someone in.

## The Pastor

For example, in the other-orientation project if someone is in pastoral training, I would tell them to host a meal and to be a servant. I would tell them to see where they can help. Perhaps they can wash the dishes. That is part of their pastoral training, is it not?

## The Evangelist

For the evangelist, I would tell them to stand in weakness and make themselves available to minister. I would tell them to be selfless in it and not to stand up and try to get recognition.

There are people that need healing and they need to minister. I would say, "Stand there and wait for the external anointing!"

Everything must be geared towards the thing that you are training them in. Do not get sidetracked by bringing up something that will distract them. If you are mentoring them into the prophetic you do not tell them that you would like to talk about the apostolic as well.

### Do Not Get Distracted

NO - Get back to the point of what you are mentoring them into. Focus. Every lesson, conversation and hurt that comes up, you gear it back to the subject at hand again and again.

Do not get distracted. By doing this, you will take them through their training quickly and efficiently.

## Step 6. The Examinations

I am going to speak briefly on the final step, which is about applying pressure and testing. There is an entire chapter on it because it is so important. Realize that you will apply pressure throughout this training.

You will need to test them to see how far they are in their training and how well they are doing. Most of the time, you will not be aware that you are giving them a test, until after you have sent the email, said the words or given the instructions.

Then you will realize that God is testing them on something. Realize that you will be testing, confronting, challenging and chiseling. See, you are not a pastor. You are a mentor. You are going to be used to shape their lives.

You cannot hide away and hope that they will get it or hope that you will maybe say the right word and it will possibly give them a conviction. No, you must be sure of what you are saying and you must give them a direct order.

Then you must step back and let the Holy Spirit do the rest.

## Summary

1.  The mentor initiates the mentorship.

2.  Define the relationship

3.  Share your expectations

4.  Send them to teachings

5.  Make your instructions specific

6.  Bring the person to the finish line through testing and pressure

7.  End mentorship

Once you have done all of these things, mentorship is over. Break the links now and let them go. Hopefully, it will go quickly if you are mentoring someone in the prophetic. In my experience, that usually lasts around nine months. Other trainings vary.

If you can follow that track through, you can take what is in you and what you have learned and you can successfully impart it to others. You can impart it in such a way that they not only rise up to your level, but also be as Elisha and take a double anointing.

Then you can see them rise up and stand in confidence. Then you can step back and let them go, knowing that you have played a part in extending the Kingdom of God.

You can sit back knowing that you have been God's vessel and that you have done what He has called all of us to do - to mentor the nations.

## The Differences Between a Mentor and Pastor

I want to take a quick interlude here and talk about the difference between a mentor and a pastor because at times this can get very confusing.

You may think that if you are the pastor or leader of a church, simply because you are working with people in your congregation, that you are mentoring them. It can be true for some relationships, but that is not always the case for everyone you are working with.

Here are some of the main differences between the two.

## Pastor Gives out Daily Bread

Firstly, the pastor gives daily bread to every believer. It is like the manna was in the Old Testament. It is what you need daily for every part of your Christian life.

We need motivation, teaching and encouragement every day. A pastor gives us this.

## Relationship With Pastor is Extended

Also, the relationship you have with the pastor is extended. It remains as long as you are a part of that church.

While you remain under that pastor, the relationship remains. The relationship with the mentor, however, is always temporary. It only lasts for the length of time that it takes to fully take on the life skill that they are mentored in.

A relationship with a pastor can be ongoing for some time. It can last anywhere from days to weeks, months and years. It depends on how long you hang around and choose to receive from them.

## Pastor Teaches on a Variety of Subjects

The pastor also teaches and counsels on daily Christian living. He handles so many varied subjects, he will teach you how to function in your marriage, how to do business God's way, flow in the gifts of the spirit so on and so forth.

His ministry is very multifaceted. You can go to your pastor and receive bits and pieces from many different subjects to help assist you in your Christian walk. It is like getting a piece of manna each day.

In mentorship, the mentor will give you one big chunk of bread. Then he will take that one chunk of bread and feed it to you until it is finished. It is not manna every day. It is just one big loaf.

## Mentorship Covers a Single Subject

It is very intense and it is on one subject alone. Because the instruction the pastor gives is so varied, you can learn many different things at a lower level. The pastor is not shaping you into something. He is simply being a leader and an example to you. He is including you in the family of God.

## The Mentor Shapes

The mentor shapes, molds and changes you. They apply a structure. A pastor would not do that. Yes, he will have a structure for his meetings, but he is not going to tell you that you cannot read something unless he tells you to.

He is not going to say, "I will mold, shape and change you", unless that pastor is mentoring another pastor. If he were mentoring another pastor, then the relationship would change.

He would say, "I am now raising you up into pastoral office and you will read what I tell you to read. You will come to these meetings and preach only when I say preach."

However, he would not speak to everyone in his congregation that way.

Perhaps, you have this problem. You have a person that looks up to you and they love you. You get on the phone, chat, share, encourage and motivate them.

You are pastoring them. It is not a mentorship relationship. Mentorship has a structure. It has a specific order and it is temporary. If such a relationship continues, it is something that can eventually turn into spiritual parenting.

 Just because you motivate and teach people, does not mean you are their mentor. You are their Pastor.

Yet, do not confuse it with mentorship. Mentorship is very clear. The person should know that they are being mentored and who their mentor is. However, we often confuse mentorship and pastoring.

You think that if you are hanging out with someone, helping them when they are down, talking about their problems, praying with them, giving them counsel and because they are looking to you as an example, that you are their mentor.

No, you are their pastor. You are fulfilling a pastoral function, not a mentorship function.

I just thought that I would add this in here because otherwise people think that they are being great mentors and mentoring everybody in their church, when they are actually pastoring them.

They are giving them daily bread, encouragement and being there when they need them. That is pastoring, not mentorship. Mentorship is very distinctive. Never forget that.

# CHAPTER 08:
# Phase 2 - Parables, Problems & Projects

> *2 Timothy 3:16 All Scripture is given by inspiration of God, and is profitable for doctrine, for reproof, for correction, for instruction in righteousness.*

I remember when I had my first disciple. I was excited, confident and as bold as any newbie prophet is. I thought that I could take on the world and that I had all the answers to save the whole world.

I jumped in with great gusto and overconfidence and said, "I am the solution to your problems. Come to me. I will be your mentor and I will show you the way to prophetic office."

It did not take very long for me to realize that it took a little bit more than guts to become a good mentor. Problems started coming up that I did not know the solutions or the correct response to.

Therefore, I did what any newly appointed prophet would do. I went on what I thought and what I felt. Moreover, I went on what I thought would work for me. The moral and outcome of the story is that I failed gloriously, because I had no clue what it meant to be a mentor.

I knew what it was to go through prophetic training for myself and I even knew what it was like to be a prophet in office. I knew how to prophesy, preach, flow in the gifts and I even had spiritual authority. However, to have these things and to impart them are two very different things.

## Knowing and Imparting are Two Different Things

Perhaps, you are today where I was back then. You may be ready to mentor and to take what you have and pour it into someone else. You have people that look up to you as their example, and you are doing exactly what I did.

You are going by what you think, what you feel and what worked for you. The problem is that it does not work that way. The foundation for their training is not based on your experience, what you think or what you feel. It is based on 2 Timothy 3:16. You forgot that the foundation of everything you are doing is the Word of God.

After you have finished reading this chapter, I want you to go and do a project for me. I want you to take the principles that I am about to share with you in this chapter. Then I want you to take one of the people that you are working with and apply each principle, step by step.

Once you have applied these principles, I want you to write down a report of how it went, how that person responded and how you felt following these principles.

Did you find it easy or difficult? Did you feel like the pressure was lifted, or did you feel you could not handle it?

After you have done that, I want you to share this with the trainer, mentor or authority that you are under.

## What Have I Just Done Here?

I have given you a parable, I have pointed out your problem and I have given you a project. These three points are essential to mentorship. If you can remember these three points and repeat them again and again, then you will always have success in mentoring.

## 1. The Parable

Although you do not use your life as a basis for the counsel you give, it is so important to use stories, illustrations and parables to reach a person. Jesus did it all the time. Read through the New Testament. He used parables.

What is a parable? It is a story that is based on real life. As I was sharing what it is like to disciple someone, if you have ever been a mentor, you could identify with at least one thing that I said.

Good - we have agreement. Now that I have your agreement and you can relate to me on this one point, I can say, "You have this problem. You are not doing it right. You are making a mistake."

A parable exposes a problem, allowing you, as a mentor, to bring the problem up and also give the solution in a way that is well received. Parables, problems and projects - these three words will be engrained in your memory by the end of this chapter.

These are the cornerstones of good mentoring. Now if we look at the scripture in 2 Timothy 3:16, he mentions four very specific functions. Those functions are teaching, conviction, restoration and training in righteousness.

I will cover training in righteousness in the next chapter. For now though I will cover the other three.

## Let's Break It Down

Paul's first three points are:

a. Teaching, which means to instruct or give parables

b. Conviction, which means to point out failures or problems

c. Restoration, which means to develop good qualities.

By giving you a project, I pull out your good qualities and I cause you to succeed. So, number one, you have gone to your disciple and you have given them a terrific track to run on. We covered that in phase one.

I said in phase one to give your disciple a track to run on, to send them to teachings and to tell them to report back to you. If you have followed that, then by now they would have come back and told you what they read, how they felt and what they thought.

## What is God Doing in Their Life?

They are going to tell you what is happening in their life. Now, what are you going to do with the information that is coming back at you? If you are a good mentor, then the first thing you are going to do is see what God is doing in their life.

If they're in pastoral training, they will probably come back and say, "I am being so challenged at home right now. The kids are getting on my case, my spouse is putting pressure on me and I cannot seem to get anything right."

What are you going to do? Are you going to say, "Do you know what your problem is? You have some bad habits. Actually, the real problem is your spouse. They are really out of line and you need to lift them up to the Lord daily, so that the Lord will convict and change them."

No - you are not going to do that. You are going to take their problems and teach them what is happening according to their training.

 Always apply your counsel to their training.

*Share the Parable*

You are going to say to them, "When I was in pastoral training, I remember how difficult it was. Pressures came on me and I could not understand why I could not even get a load of laundry done during the day."

They will think, "I so understand you." Then you can say, "Can you not see that you are going through the same challenges in your life that I did? Can't you see that these circumstances are part of your training?"

Then you can teach them in and take them as a mother would a child and point things out. You can say, "Can't you see that this is your training here? Can you see that God is doing this in your life?"

If you are working with a prophet, you would say, "Can you see that God is bringing your will, emotions, weaknesses and strengths to death? Can you see in this particular circumstance that "this" is what God is doing?"

## Pointing Out Markers

You will teach and instruct. By doing that, it will be as if you are pointing out markers along the road for them. Is that not what a mentor is there to do? The Holy Spirit puts their feet on the road. You cannot do that.

They must "get on the bus" and start the road with the help of the Holy Spirit. However, what you can do is show them the countryside along the way. You can say, "Do you see that? This is what that means…"

I remember when I was in Switzerland and we went on a long drive with a couple that was hosting us. They took us on a tour and explained everything to us. They would say, "Do you see that mountain? That is the Niederhorn. Do you see this mountain that we are passing by? That is the Jungfrau." Then they would also explain the history of it.

They would say, "Do you see that little town? Do you see that lake?" Then they would share a story, even some myths and parables. They took us to this one mountain and told us that they still believe in dragons and that there was a lot of mythology surrounding it.

It was fascinating. I could drive that route again and know a lot about where I was and where we were going. When we had to drive that road by ourselves, we immediately identified the landmarks.

### Preparing for the Future

If you are a good mentor, pointing out these things to your disciple prepares them for the future. When the time comes for your disciple to rise up and mentor others, they will recognize the road because you made it very clear for them along the way.

Never forget that you are there to impart, teach and instruct. You have sent them to the teachings, which is great. The teachings have challenged, convicted and brought them to a place of being open to receive.

However, that is not good enough. You need to take what they have learned and apply it to their lives for right now. You need to take that word and make it into a rhema word for them.

You need to say, "This is not just something that God said through this author ten years ago. This is something that God is saying to you right now through these teachings. Can't you see that God is challenging you in this area?"

If someone is in evangelistic training, you can say, "Can't you see that God is bringing this area of your flesh to death? Can you see that these pressures are coming upon you, so that you will let go of your control, strengths and abilities?"

You need to apply it and you are only going to do that by teaching and instructing. What better way is there to teach and instruct than by using parables?

### As Simple as Toothpicks

I remember when my daughter, Jessica, started to really become fascinated with mathematics. She learned that there was something called fractions. So she went to her father and said, "Dad, can you teach me about fractions?"

Being the loving father that he is, he sat down with a bunch of toothpicks and he broke them up and told her a whole story about how breaking them up makes them into halves, quarters and so on.

Before you knew it, there were toothpicks all over the table. I could not believe how much she paid attention and how much she retained. She got the concept immediately. All he did was take something as simple as toothpicks.

By breaking them up, showing the concept to her practically and telling her stories, she understood immediately. That is how we should be teaching and instructing. I am not talking about standing up and saying, "Thus says the Lord... one, two, three, etc."

I am talking about using real life examples, just like I used with you. It all comes back to being a leader and using the art of communication. You will have to be real. You have to have lived life. You will need to understand.

### I Understand

You cannot stand up and say, "I am going to call your flesh to death. I have never had that problem, so I cannot relate to you at all. Regardless... you must just deal with it."

What kind of mentor is that? The Scriptures say that the Lord was tempted in all the same things that we are tempted in. He was tested and can identify with us. The book of Hebrews says that we do not have someone that has not suffered or gone through trials. (Heb 4:15)

We have someone who has been tested and experienced what we have experienced. When He says, "I understand," you know that He understands. That is why He could stand up and share the parables that He did.

He lived them and they were real. If you cannot be real, then you have not even got a foot in the door of being a good mentor because being a good mentor means being real. In order to apply teaching, you must take normal, real, daily things and make them alive in the heart of your disciple.

## 2. Problems

However, it is not just all about teachings. It is great to hear stories. I can sit and listen to stories all the time. When Craig was sharing with Jessica about fractions, he did not just sit and instruct her.

After teaching her, he pulled the toothpicks together and started to question her a bit. He said, "What does this make?" Sometimes she got it right and sometimes she got it wrong.

Whenever she got it wrong, he said, "That is not correct. You have come to a wrong conclusion. You think that these two quarters make a whole, but they only make a half. Can't you see that these ones are smaller? Can you not see that they do not line up?"

Then she would say, "Aha. I see."

Then he would show her something else and say, "Now, tell me what this makes."

She would say, "This makes a half. This makes a whole." Suddenly, she could understand fractions.

However, it was not good enough just to get the story, parable or illustration. She also needed the correction when she missed it. It is great to instruct and teach. Yet, if you do not point out the problems, then your disciples will not take any steps forward.

### Is Conviction Enough?

What is conviction? It is when you do a full one hundred and eighty degree turn. When you are going one direction then you stop and turn around and go the opposite direction.

It is fine and well to get a conviction, but if I am just standing and facing the new direction and not moving forward, then I am still not walking out my calling in righteousness, am I? I need to take a step forward.

It takes more than a conviction. It takes more than just saying, "Aha. I see." Now what is the next step? You cannot just give a parable and leave it at the point when they see that it applies to them.

All they will do is think that it is fascinating and interesting, and then they will go and think about it some more.

### Don't Leave Them Hanging

If you are a good mentor, you won't leave it there. You will drive in the nail and put the spear in the side. You will bring conviction and death and you will point out the problems.

It is up to you to bring your disciple to conviction. No conviction, no change.

Why? You will do this because that is what makes you a good mentor. It is not good enough just to say to your disciple, "I am glad that you got a conviction for your bitterness."

They come to you and say, "I listened to the *At Liberty to Love* teaching and I was so convicted. The Lord really pointed these things out to me."

My response? "I remember working with a person that received the same conviction as you. She realized that she did not just have bitterness towards her husband, but that this bitterness started years ago.

However, only once she dealt with the root of that bitterness and received inner healing did she really break free. I see that with you too. You have that same kind of problem. You think that your bitterness is just with your husband, but actually your bitterness is much deeper than that.

Now, you must face that root, see that this is sin and stop seeing yourself as a victim. Instead of wallowing, you must rise up and take the sword that God has given you and deal with this problem. If you don't do that, then you will never rise up."

## Pull Out the Problems

See, it is not good enough to say, "I am so glad that you got a conviction". They have a conviction, but now you must push them in the right direction. Pull out the problems.

I think eighty percent of being a mentor is pulling out people's problems. You are like a gem cutter. What does the cutter see when he looks at a diamond? He does not just see the diamond, but he sees all its flaws.

I guarantee that if you talk to anyone that is in some type of artisan trade, not matter what it is, the first thing that they will look at is the quality of the piece.

They might say, "Do you see that? The artisan did not do a good enough job there."

"Do you see that? They messed up there."

If you go to a hairdresser, they will do the same thing. They will say, "Who cut your hair the last time you had it done?"

You say, "Sarah, why?"

Then they say, "I was wondering because I see that they really did not know how to do layers very well. This side is longer than that side."

When a specialist looks at a work, they always see the things that need to be fixed because that is their job. As a mentor, do not be afraid to look at the things that need to be fixed.

### The Good, the Bad and the Ugly

It is true that we must see the beauty. If we did not see the beauty, we would not even start our job in the first place. However, realize that unless you look at the flaws and are prepared to look at both the good and bad, you are useless as a mentor.

Anyone can go and ask the Lord in a journal about what their good qualities are. It does not even take a fantastic revelation to get that. However, it does take a mentor to expose the weakness and the flaws, and then bring change.

You can walk around with a problem and a specific template that is destroying your life and not know that it is there. Look at your own life as an illustration. How many times have you gone through situations and not known that you were triggering all along to a hurt of the past?

Your past has shaped the way that you think in the present. It has shaped the way that you treat people and the way you minister. It took one person to come and say, "Do you know that you have this problem? Do you know that you have such a victim mentality that you blame everyone in the world for your failures? Your failure in life is your own fault."

## Use the Word as a Sword

It allows you to see yourself in a mirror of truth. However, a mentor should not just leave it there. They should take you to true restoration. I also want to mention that when bringing conviction, you must always use the Word.

When you bring conviction or you are exposing problems in people, you must use the Word. Using personal illustrations is great when you are teaching and instructing. I am not saying to set yourself up as a standard, but to use stories to get your point across.

However, when you come to apply counsel or correction, you have to use the Word of God. You cannot say, "That is not acceptable to me because I say so."

"The Lord told me that it was not good enough for me, so then it is also not good enough for you."

You cannot do that. Why is bitterness wrong? It is wrong because the Scriptures say that it is like wormwood and it defiles many. (Heb 12:15) The sin of witchcraft is unacceptable in the Word and if it is unacceptable in the Word, then it is unacceptable to me.

Use the Word. You can always back up what you say by the Word of God. Once you have brought that conviction, give them a project. You cannot just say, "You are full of sin." You have to tell them what to do.

## 3. Project

Now you cannot just cut someone open expose that person's guts and say, "Have a nice day. See you next week." You have to give them some kind of closure.

You have to give them a project now that you have exposed their problem.

You will have to get revelation and use wisdom for this step. If you really want to receive what I have and mentor as I do, then you better open your heart and expect to pick up the anointing as you are reading this book, because knowing what project to apply takes spiritual revelation.

This is spiritual wisdom, which I cannot give you a three-step process for. I cannot tell you what projects I will give someone. I can have two people come to me with the same problem, same sin and even the same root and I will give them two different projects.

## You Need Revelation

How do I come up with the projects? I get them by revelation. The Lord will give me a vision, a word of knowledge or a word of wisdom. I cannot tell you how to give a project or what the best way to word it is. That comes from spiritual wisdom.

However, there are some standard ones. For example, if someone comes to you with bitterness, there is a good bitterness project. Go through all the people you are bitter with and write down their names.

You can say, "Go and do that project and report back to me". There are some projects that are good for everyone to do. However, you are going to have to get revelation and allow the Holy Spirit to tell you what they need.

Tell them to dig in the Word. If they have a conflict with someone, then their project is going to be to go and resolve that conflict.

 Add spiritual wisdom to the naturalistic mentorship abilities.

   **Tools of the Trade**

I gave you a project at the beginning of this chapter. I told you to go through these principles, take one of the conversations that you have had with a recent disciple and to apply the three points.

You need to give them a parable, point out a problem and give them a project. Now that is your project. As you do it, if you start from the top down, then it will be obvious what they need to do.

Trust me - it will be obvious, especially if you are in a fivefold office. You will know already what you were expected to do when you were in a certain situation and that is a good place to start.

# CHAPTER 09:
# Fivefold Ministry Mentorship

The principles that I have shared so far can be used for any level of mentorship, whether it is naturalistic or spiritual.

However, for the fivefold ministry offices, there are distinct differences that I would like to take a moment to point out to you.

So depending on who you are training, the teachings you give them as well as the level at which you train will vary.

## Getting Your Ministries Straight

I have seen a lot of confusion with mixing up ministry roles, which is why I want to touch on it in this chapter. I have seen apostles calling pastors to apostolic deaths and I have seen apostles think that the deaths they have to go through for apostolic training will be the same as the deaths in pastoral training.

The death to the flesh that God calls us to experience for each ministry is different. It is just like having a position in the world. Depending on the position you apply for, will determine the responsibility that you carry, the salary you get, the training you must go through and what is expected of you.

A CEO does not come into work much later than everyone else. He is expected to work harder, to know more, to have more wisdom and have more answers. He is expected to be superhuman. It is what the staff expects from him.

However, if the janitor makes a mistake, who really notices it? He can get away with a lot more than someone in a higher position. It is the same with the fivefold ministry offices. You cannot apply the same pressures and the same expectation to all of the fivefold.

## The Pressures of Apostolic Training

The apostle is the highest of all fivefold offices. Therefore, he has the hardest training. He will be challenged in the spiritual and the natural and he is not allowed to get away with anything.

If he is in the flesh anywhere, if there is sin, if there is a bad attitude, if he woke up feeling bad or even if his hair is a mess, it is unacceptable.

It never fails to amaze me how an apostle in training can send me a good letter and I will correct, chisel and plunge the dagger in his heart. I sit back and think, "The poor guy got challenged again."

It is because the apostle holds the highest responsibility in the body of Christ and if he is to hold such a great responsibility then he better shape up to it. He is expected to communicate more, teach better, preach better, know the Word more, prophesy better and have more authority.

He is not allowed to have sin, failures or bad days. If he is asked to write a letter in five minutes, I do not care if he is having a bad day and if the whole world is on his shoulders, he better do it.

There is no place for mistakes or errors, because you are an apostle. As a mentor, I put a lot pressure on an apostle in training. Whether they excel or fail does not matter. The reality is that the pressure is what will change them and make them into that vessel that the Lord needs them to be.

If I let them go their own way, then what kind of person or apostle would they become? They would be someone that says, "Oh well. It is just somebody's life or just another church that I have messed up - who cares?"

From the beginning, I have to let them know, without a doubt, the intensity and how big the responsibility is that they are carrying. How else can I do it? Other than by applying that pressure to them myself? (By the leading of the Holy Spirit of course)

How else can I bring change than by saying, "I do not like it this way. I want more from you. I expect more from you."

When I am no longer there, they are going to get it directly from the Lord. So I am preparing them for what is to come. I cannot let them get away with anything.

I cannot let them get away with, "I am sorry that I forgot to write to you. I will get around to it next week." Oh really? I may let a pastor get away with that, but I will never ever let an apostle get away with that.

It is unacceptable. Push harder. Try harder. Die harder. Welcome to apostolic training. If you do not like it, then get off the bus. I have no sympathy for an apostle in training. It is the highest office and to whom much is given, much is required of. Never forget that.

## The Pressures of Prophetic Training

The prophet carries the same type of training, but not quite as intense as the apostle. For the apostle, I will be there, to a certain degree, to meet their need for recognition, but they are still expected to have a strong enough relationship with the Lord, that I do not have to meet those needs anymore.

I assume that they already have a close relationship with the Lord, so I am now shaping and training their characters to be more effective. Yet, with the prophet it is not so. They will have a very strong need for acceptance and recognition.

As a mentor, you need to try and meet that need - although not entirely. Most of your time with that disciple will be spent challenging those needs and bringing it to their attention, so that they can have that relationship with the Lord.

They will be called to death in every area of their soul. Their mind, will and emotions, along with their weaknesses and strengths will be called to death. It is up to you to expose those needs.

The prophetic training is one wrought with challenges. You will find yourself not necessarily slamming them and bringing a hammer on their head, but you will be challenging them. You will say, "Do you really think you can do this? Do you really want to do this?"

"Are you prepared to die again and again and be nothing for Christ if He asks you to?" You will and should continue to pressure them with challenges. Prophets love it. They will thrive. If you challenge a prophet, they will rise to that challenge.

You will say, "Do you want to pray? Do you really think that you want to pray? Then you better get into the Word because until you get into the Word, you will not be effective." The next thing you know, they will be studying the Word.

Next you will say to them, "Do you want to rise up in authority? Do you want to speak with fire? Then you can be sure you will be facing seasons of death. There is going to be death to the flesh, death to your will and death to your need to be in control. If you want the power, then that is the price."

## The Pressures of Teacher Training

However, it is not necessary to call a teacher to death in the same way. If you say that to a teacher, he will look at you and say, "You can have it. I am going to sit here and read my bible. Leave me alone."

A teacher needs to be challenged to step out in confidence, because a teacher needs to be confident in the Scriptures and in their revelations. However, they are not required to die at an apostolic level.

With a teacher, their deaths will come automatically because their training will revolve all around their mind, their revelations and their thinking. They are going to get into deception and mess up.

I have discovered through personal experience that the teacher is probably the most left alone disciple of all the fivefold. As they go through things, you as a mentor will pick it up and say, "Do you see that you just got into deception there?"

Sometimes you may say, "Have you got into this teaching?" You will be there simply to steer and guide them. It is not very often that you will have to bring a teacher to death, unless they get into deception or some old ideas come up.

The most challenging thing you will do to a teacher in their training is to expose their old foundations and to bring a rod to them, as Paul spoke about. He brings a rod of correction.

You are to shatter their old teaching foundations and bring them to a place of confusion. Therefore, many of your conversations will be, "Did you see this in the Word? What do you think about that? Do you know what you taught here does not line up with this?"

You will challenge them in this way. Also, you will say, "Where did you get that doctrine from? That doctrine is not based on the Word. You picked up that doctrine from someone who was not even spirit filled."

You just slammed their foundation. You hit them with the truth. You hit them with the sword of the spirit. By doing that, you will challenge every single thing that they believe. Your job is to challenge the mind of a teacher, continuously.

You cannot challenge them like you would a prophet and say, "Do you want the power? Die already!"

He will say, "I do not want that. Leave me alone." A teacher does not want that type of fire.

He does not want the glory like a prophet and he does not continually say, "Kill me more Lord!"

Also, you cannot challenge a teacher in the way you would an apostle. It would crush him and demoralize him.

He is not at that level of training. You must challenge what he believes. His entire doctrinal foundation must be challenged, because by the end of his training he will be at a point where he will not know what he believes anymore.

Everything that he has tried has failed. Therefore, the best thing that you can do for the teacher is to give him projects. Then as he tries his best to do every project perfectly, he will fail in nearly every single one.

You will say, "Get into a study of this passage and see what you come up with." He will either get into deception or realize that everything that he believed is wrong and it will bring him to death. Then, he will have to let go.

Next, you will send him to go read a book, and tell him to apply all the principles and none of them will work. For the first time in his life, nothing will work.

That is the training of a teacher. God strips you entirely of what you thought, believed and firmly stood up for, until you are nothing. Then He will build you up with a fresh foundation.

This happens so that when you stand up and teach, you teach from experience as well as from the Word and with the anointing from the Spirit and not from your own puffed up revelations. Do you see how you cannot give the same challenges to each one?

## The Pressures of Pastoral Training

Then we have the pastor. The problem is that we have too many prophets trying to mentor pastors. Prophets are continually calling them to death. It is the pastor that leads the sheep. He is the nice, loving guy.

You do not train a pastor by chiseling him every five minutes. You are there to meet the need of acceptance in this disciple, one hundred percent. You have to represent the Lord to them, so that they know what He looks like in order for them to present that image to the sheep.

You encourage, motivate and point things out along the way. You will find yourself doing a lot of counseling and instructing. So you better be good at that.

You are going to send them to the right materials to learn how to deal with problems. They are going to have people coming to them and you will have to teach them how to counsel.

You are going to teach them to have what we call an "other-orientation". You will have to teach them to pour out. Again, you will give them lots of projects. However, when they fail, you do not say, "That is it. You just failed the test and you will never be a pastor. Get lost!"

No. You do that to a prophet because he is the only one that will say, "I refuse to accept that. I am still going all the way." A pastor will give up because they are in pastoral training and there is an entirely different kind of training.

You have to push them forward with motivation, not with a challenge. You have to give encouragement and exhortation. Yet, you also cannot be afraid to point out any mistakes you see.

Give good teaching based on the Word and lots of storytelling. Say things like, "Did you know that you need to do that?" Sometimes that is all you need to do, in order to bring a pastor to a place of conviction.

Projects are the best course of training for the pastor, because those in pastoral office work with a lot more people up close. They work with a variety of people who are all at a different level of spiritual maturity. Therefore, they need a lot of projects. Also, the great thing is that you can include so many different kinds of materials.

The pastor does a little bit of everything. It is a very widespread ministry. If someone is in pastoral training, I will not send that person to read *Prophetic Boot Camp*, which is a resource, more for the prophet.

I would send them to books like *Today's Pastor*, *How to Get People to Follow You* and lots of other teachings because they should have a very widespread understanding of all the fivefold.

## The Pressures of Evangelistic Training

Lastly, we have the evangelist. Now, if you are training up an evangelist, you are not going to say, "I accept your sinful flesh. I understand. No one else may understand you, but I understand that you are full of sin. I accept you and I want to motivate you to really press through and touch the Lord and really understand the Lord Jesus."

No, this is an evangelist we are dealing with here. For an evangelist, you are continually addressing the sins of the flesh. You are emphasizing a relationship with the Holy Spirit and the external anointing.

You should be very hard, sharp and direct. On the other hand, you should always be there for them. You do not challenge an evangelist like you would a prophet. You tell an evangelist what to do. You call them to death.

You say, "This is unacceptable and that is unacceptable. Deal with it!" What you will find interesting is that with the evangelist you will not find yourself addressing many of his spiritual problems, because somebody who was just born again yesterday can immediately start flowing in the evangelistic.

It is not about his spiritual maturity. What God is going to deal with in the evangelist is his righteousness, his holiness, as it is traditionally preached. God is going to deal with the sin in his life or the problems in his life.

If he is still smoking and drinking, you are going to address that. You will really address the natural things, whereas with the prophet, you are really dealing with the soul, the spirit and the roots.

With the evangelist, you may deal with the roots of the flesh, but not as deeply as you would with the higher offices. You are going to deal with the obvious things because once the training comes, the Holy Spirit is going to level them down so much that the flesh and the soul will not be much of a problem after all that.

You are going to challenge everything that they are good and successful at. That is what you are going to cut down. You will find that a lot of your challenges will be naturalistic but not on his understanding of the Word.

If you call him to death on his doctrine, he will not care. Do not send an evangelist to learn tons of doctrine. He does not care. You cannot say, "The problem with you is that you do not know doctrine."

Just think about this logically for a moment. He is an evangelist. Of course, he does not know tons of doctrine. He just knows the basics. He knows enough though to stand and be used of God. He knows enough to have a relationship with the Holy Spirit.

You should be challenging him to have a relationship with the Holy Spirit and by doing that you are also going to challenge all of the naturalistic things in his life.

Therefore, you cannot challenge him like you would an apostle. You cannot try to get him to flow in the internal anointing. You cannot say, "The problem is that you need to 'feel' the word of wisdom and 'sense' what is going on in the spirit."

No. An evangelist flows in the external anointing, not the internal anointing. You cannot tell an evangelist to sit and get visions and tap into his spirit. He is an evangelist. It is about a relationship with the Holy Spirit and he will hear things very differently. He will hear the clear voice of the Holy Spirit and will receive distinct direction.

You should challenge him by saying, "What are you doing sitting there thinking for? Step out in faith! I do not care what you feel. Step out in the external anointing and in faith and it will come."

I love flowing in the prophetic. It is so comfortable for me. I can sit there and tap into my spirit and the wisdom just bubbles up. When it comes to the evangelist all of that dies. You wonder what to do and debate on stepping out because you do not "feel" anything.

If you are an evangelist, then I do not care what you feel or think - you just need to step out. However, when you stand up there empty and not knowing what to say or do, the anointing will suddenly come.

That is how it works for the evangelist. You need to apply that pressure in order to bring them to that place. Are you starting to see a clear picture on how you are to work with your disciples?

## The Core Principles of Training Remain the Same

Take those three points. Share stories, expose things and give them projects. However, do it in line with the training that you are giving them. I know that as you work with different offices, you will come back to this chapter and go over it again and again.

Let us bring it all to a conclusion now. Give your teaching, your parable, point out the problems and give your projects. You will apply this over and over again.

As your disciple comes back to you with a teaching, you will challenge them and send them away with a project to either go through more teachings or to do something practical. Then they will come back to you and you will repeat the same process again.

This can go on for a series of months. In the next chapter, we will take a look at the fourth part. I will teach you a bit about discipline, bringing your disciple to death and how to use the chisel effectively.

I touched on it a bit in this chapter, but it is going to come up more and more, especially in the higher ministry offices. You will want to know how to actually bring somebody to death.

How do you bring them to the cross? How do you take them through to resurrection? Does it just happen? Does the Holy Spirit do it? Do you step back? You wish.

You will come to understand this wonderful experience of having a chisel in your hand and a hammer on your head! We will discuss this in more detail in the next chapter.

# CHAPTER 10:
# Phase 3: Chiseling and Correction

## Shaping and Sculpting

I love anything related to the arts and creativity. In my spare time, I love to do artistic things. One time, I had the opportunity to learn some drawing.

The opportunity came up to do something new and I got into pencil drawing. It was such a wonderful experience. I came across this technique where you took your sheet of paper and charcoaled in the whole page.

Then, you looked at the object or picture that you wanted to draw and you took an eraser and bit-by-bit you took out all the pieces of light that you saw on your image.

No matter what you were looking at, whether it was a bowl of fruit or a person's face, instead of trying to draw the direct image you would start with taking out the pieces of light on the picture you wanted to draw.

Once you brought out all the pieces of light, you then took your pencil and shaded in all the dark pieces that were darker than the original shading you did in the beginning. By a process of simply taking some charcoal out and darkening other portions, I was amazed to find a 3D image popping out from the page.

What was once a blank piece of paper with charcoal smudged neatly over it was now a 3D image that I had drawn. It was such a fantastic experience. As I came to look at the process of mentorship, especially the topic of shaping and chiseling, it reminded me of the process I went through in learning to draw.

Correcting and mentoring is pretty much like that style of drawing. When a person comes to you, they are very much like that charcoal that was smudged all over the page. They have a lot of stuff in their lives.

 Mentoring means shaping through removing from and adding to your disciple.

## You Need to Both Add and Take Away

Some of that stuff needs to be removed. At the same time though, there is a lot of stuff missing that you will need to add. In the process of taking things away and adding other things to them, you will start to shape them.

When you look at someone's life, to you it may seem like a bunch of smudges or bits and pieces scattered all over. However, by the time you are finished you will have molded that person into something that God wanted them to be.

## Training in Righteousness

In the last chapter, I spoke about the first few things in 2 Tim. 3:16. Remember I mentioned that we would talk about training in righteousness in the next chapter? Well, that is exactly what we will look at now, because that encapsulates everything about chiseling and correction.

## Training

Chiseling and correction are quite vital parts of the mentorship process. I did a little studying on the word "training in righteousness." When I looked up the word "training" in the Greek, it came up as "paideia".

It also gave me some other synonyms for the word. The synonyms listed are: chastening, instruction and chastisement. It went on to speak a bit about how it refers to the education of children relating to cultivation of minds and morals.

You might think training involves a lot of fun and simple instruction, but then words like chastisement and chastening are used. These two words do not sound like a lot of fun!

To be an effective mentor, it is going to take more than just teaching someone the principles. This training is all about action – not just instruction and knowledge.

## Righteousness

You chastise and mold. However, being a good mentor is not just all about chastisement – the full phrase is "training in righteousness."

When I looked up the word "righteousness" it showed me the Greek word "dikaiosune".

"Dikaiosune" is the common word used for righteousness in Scripture. It's meaning is simply, "To be in right standing with God." Another translation used, that I love is, "The condition acceptable to God".

So when we are looking at the phrase, "Training in righteousness", in essence what it is saying is that chastisement or chiseling is needed to make you acceptable to God.

Pressure and training are needed to challenge and change a person until they become acceptable to God.

What is and is not acceptable will change from person to person depending on their spiritual maturity and what level of training you have called them to. Never forget though that chastisement is a big part of the process.

In our ministry at A.M.I. we call that chastisement a "chisel".

It is like the drawing I spoke about in the beginning or like a sculptor taking away the pieces of stone to bring out a beautiful carving. It has a purpose. You do not just take a piece of paper and start rubbing things out and scratching things in randomly - hoping that something will come of it.

### *You Are God's Artist*

There has to be a purpose. The goal, according to the Word, is to bring them to a condition that is acceptable to God. You are to chastise, chisel and correct until they become something righteous.

You are molding them. You are an artist in the hand of God. You are His paintbrush, His chisel, and His vessel. You are meant to shape the person you are training. Why is this necessary?

Think about it. When did you change the most? Think about the times in your life when you were put in a situation where you had no other choice but to change. If you have not yet experienced such a changing experience, by the end of this chapter you will start experiencing it!

 You cannot avoid bringing pressure. It is vital to the process.

Pressure is what brings change. Perhaps, you are in a position with a boss that is the meanest, loudest and most arrogant man that you have ever met. You are forced to work more efficiently and to do things that you never thought you could do before.

Even when that boss left, you were still capable of doing the job. Why is that? It's because pressure was put on you until you changed. As a mentor, you must put pressure in the right place.

However, you cannot just jump around and put pressure wherever you want. Pressure will bring out qualities and cause your disciple to be molded and shaped until they come to a condition that is acceptable to God.

They are not to become acceptable to you, but to God. There is a very big difference. You are to correct, discipline and bring the person into a place of being what God wants them to be.

That really sums up this entire chapter. You need to bring them to a place, of what God wants them to be according to the Word. It may seem obvious to you to shape them into what God wants them to be, but it is not as clear as you think!

The truth is, when you start working with a person, the first thing that will come up will be all your preconceived ideas and the things that you think that you need to make them into.

Never forget that if you are a mentor, you are meant to be making people into what God wants, not what you want.

You are molding your disciple into God's image – not yours.

## Using the Chisel

So when do you use the chisel? When you feel like it? When you think it is a good idea? I am not going to get overly spiritual here. I am going to lay it on the line and tell you the truth. I am going to tell you when I chisel the most.

I chisel the most when I feel the emotion rising up from within me. When the Lord is leading me, He leads through my emotions. When did Jesus correct and chisel His disciples?

Take a look at Mark 9:19. It says,

> *He answered him and said, "O faithless generation, how long shall I be with you? How long shall I bear with you? Bring him to Me."*

He was basically saying, "For goodness sakes guys, how much longer do I have to bear with this?"

His disciples had come to Him with a child that was having fits and they tried to cast the demon out, but they could not do it. So they brought him to Jesus. The man said, "Your disciples tried to pray, but they could not cast the demon out."

Now, instead of Jesus saying, "I understand. I know it is difficult," he said, "For goodness sakes guys, how much longer must I bear with you?" Read through the gospels and see how many times Jesus had to say that to them.

He said it again and again. Mark 8:32 talks about Jesus sharing with His disciples how He was going to die. Then Peter jumped in with his big mouth and the Scriptures say that Peter rebuked Jesus for saying what He did.

What did Jesus do after this? Did He stand there and say, "Father, tell me how I should respond to Peter at this time. What is the word Lord?"

This is what Jesus said in Mark 8:33,

> *But when He had turned around and looked at His disciples, He rebuked Peter, saying, "Get behind Me, Satan! For you are not mindful of the things of God, but the things of men."*

Jesus did not stand there waiting for revelation. Peter said the wrong thing at the wrong time and he paid the consequences thereof. In a split second, Jesus turned around and said, "Get behind me, satan. You do not have a clue what you are talking about."

Jesus was very quick with His mouth. He was quick to rebuke the fig tree and quick to rebuke His disciples. He did not ponder or dwell on it day upon day. When the fig tree did not have fruit, He did not sit there contemplating about how the seeds should be germinating or how long they should germinate for.

He just got upset with the fig tree and told it to die. It was very quick, simple and effective. Jesus treated His disciples like this often.

## When to Chisel

So when are you going to chisel? You will know when it is time to chisel because your disciple will write to you or say something that will infuriate you. It won't infuriate you personally though.

It will infuriate you because they missed it and because it is against the Word of God and everything that the Lord and the Word stands for. They might write something like, "I know I am deeply bitter with my mother, but how can you blame me? She was such a horrible woman that treated me like this, this and this. Therefore, I am justified in my bitterness toward her."

This is what they should get in response from you, "You know what? Do not ever write me such a letter. Do not ever write to me and tell me that you are full of bitterness and ask me to just 'understand' you.

The Word of God does neither understand you nor comprehend your bitterness. It is against the Word of God and against everything that God stands for. Therefore, do not come to me with your bitterness and expect me to 'understand'.

I am not going to 'understand' because the Word of God does not understand. The blood that Jesus shed does not understand. Instead it tells us to love our enemies and to lay our lives down for one another."

Do you want a chisel? You can trigger a chisel in me very quickly by standing against what the Word says.

Do not come and give me self-pity or say that you "do not have a conviction" about a certain sin. If you want conviction, come to me and I will smack you with the Word of God.

Do not come to me and say that you do not have conviction. If you do not have it, then go and get a conviction. Whether you have a conviction or not, the Word of God says that hatred against anyone is sin and that you are out of line to dwell on it.

You have to know the Word and be convicted of the Word yourself though. That way when someone comes to you and presents to you their flesh and sin, your first reaction is a righteous anger.

## A Problem With Being the Chisel

However, there can be a problem here sometimes.

Perhaps you had a leader that chiseled you in this way. Perhaps you had someone over you, who put you down and you still feel hurt and rejected. You may have said to yourself, "When I work with someone, I am not going to be like that. I remember how tough it was to get those chisels. I remember how devastating it was to get those corrections.

Therefore, when I am in charge and I am the mentor, I am not going to do that. I am not going to apply that pressure that I received. I am going to be gracious."

Do you know what you just did there? You just said, "Yes Lord, I will do your will, but..."

### No Yes... Buts

How gracious do you think Jesus was when He braided those leather strips and whipped the moneychangers? You can thank the Lord for every chisel and correction that you have received because it has made you into the vessel that you are now.

You should thank the Lord for every dominating, arrogant leader that pressured you, because they pressured you into the person that you are right now. Without that pressure and correction, you would not be in the position to pour out what you have because it would not have been poured out to you.

 Watch out for your "blind spots" when bringing discipline.

So do not deny your disciple the opportunity for the same growth and promotion. When you say, "I am not going to apply the pressure the same way it was put on me. I am going to be different."

Firstly, you are showing bitterness against the person that applied those pressures to you. Secondly, you have given the Lord a "yes, but." With this attitude, you may as well say goodbye to your whole ministry.

### The Blind Spot

Then thirdly, you are robbing your disciple of the opportunity to grow. This is called a "blind spot." You overlook your disciple's sins because you did not like it when someone addressed yours.

If Jesus was not afraid of conflict, then why should you be? God didn't allow sin in any way. Ask Achan and his family about how the Father treated sin. The ground swallowed them up. Ask Joshua what God thought about sin. He made the Israelites wander in the desert for forty years, until every last one had died before Joshua could even put foot on the land.

Do you think I am being overly strong in my statements? This is easy compared to what the Word of God says. Do you want the truth? The truth is that we serve a very righteous God. He cannot bear the sight of sin. On the other hand though, we also have a loving Savior that understands us.

If you want to stand up, be an example, take what you have and impart it to others, then you better be a righteous vessel that is acceptable to God first before you start shooting off your mouth.

You better have walked through the fire and you better be prepared to allow others to walk through the fire as well to get to this place. Stop squirming and complaining about how tough it is, because not only is it going to get tougher for you, but it is also your responsibility to make it tough for your disciples.

## Why Chiseling is Needed

When you bring pressure, you are not doing it to be unfair or out of your own selfishness. Rather, you are taking them through the correct fire at the correct time to bring out the treasure that is within. You owe it to them.

If you cannot bring pressure then they could just as well read the Word, find the truth for themselves and forget about you being their mentor. What is the use of you being there, if you are not going to say anything?

I told you this before and I am going to tell you again. Being a trainer is 80% seeing the wrong and 20% healing and impartation, which I will talk about in the next chapters.

The impartation is the easy part. I can stand up at a conference and impart everything that I have to everyone. It is easy. I can give you the anointing, wisdom and the teaching. I can instruct you and even pray for inner healing. That takes five minutes.

## Dealing with Blockages Takes Time

However, removing templates, sins and obstacles that prevent you from receiving the impartation will take time. The mindsets, sinful habit patterns and demonic spiritual DNA that you received from your generations have to be dealt with.

These are things that will prevent you from receiving the healing and the anointing. Eighty percent of any training is about removing the veils. The impartation is instantaneous.

I identified this when I first started working with the prophets. I found that when I imparted any of the gifts to them, their manifestation was immediate. They started operating in those gifts exactly like me, immediately.

The gift of discerning of spirits was the first. They would sense oppression and the anointing in the exact same way I did. They would see visions the way that I saw them. They would have dreams the way I had dreams.

I also saw this with my husband, Craig. Right after he was led him to the Lord, we prayed and within two weeks of being saved, he was flowing in diverse tongues and prophecy.

 Impartation is easy if you remove the hindrances first.

Impartation is easy. You are wondering why you are not moving forward. You are wondering why you do not have the anointing that you want. It is not about the anointing. There is no problem with the anointing.

## Hindrances to the Anointing

The problems are the obstacles and walls that are preventing you from receiving the anointing. That is why I am continually saying in this chapter that you must first pull out the problems and then challenge and deal with the issues.

You have to deal with the templates, wield the chisel and bring correction when it is needed because when you do that, then they will be able to receive the anointing. When you deal with those things, the impartation is almost immediate.

If they are looking up to you already, then it is even easier. They will start acting like you and they will immediately receive what you have. This can be both a good or bad thing, depending on your spiritual condition.

# CHAPTER 11:
# How to Chisel

In the last chapter I used an example in which I shared about your disciple coming and telling you that they are bitter because of how their mother treated them. When a situation like this comes up, you have a choice to make. Are you going to follow through or let it go?

If there is a personal sin or character flaw that you see the Lord exposing in them at that moment, then the choice is quite clear. It is time to get involved!

You should be very much like Jesus when He turned to Peter and said, "Get thee behind me, satan. You are thinking about the things of men, instead of the things of God."

## 1. The Perfect Time – When It Comes Up

This attitude is unacceptable. It is not right for your disciple to expect you to be sorry for their bitterness. You have to address it immediately. You cannot go away and wait. The Lord has this person on a very clear track for their training and if this thing is coming up now, then God wants you to deal with it now.

Look for the signs. Look at what they do and do not say. If they are doing something that is against the Word or doing something that you feel in your spirit is unacceptable, then now is the time to address it.

You cannot wait for a better moment. In fact, these things usually come up at the most inconvenient times. The last thing you will feel like doing is chiseling, but that is the time to deal with it. God has brought it up for a purpose.

You may say something to them that causes them to spew at you without even realizing it was going to affect them. That is good. It is a good time to apply the chisel right there.

You cannot wait because when you wait, the Lord has to arrange another set of circumstances so that they can spew at you again and then you can correct it. You will delay their training by not addressing it when you should.

## 2. Use the Word When you Chisel

The most powerful tool that you can use as a chisel is the Word of God. It is so powerful. I like to use the bitterness illustration because everyone has that one. No matter the training this usually always comes up, so that is why I am using this example continually.

If somebody comes to me with bitterness, I tell that person, "The Word says that bitterness is like wormwood. It defiles many. It defiles your ministry, family and even you. It is as the sin of witchcraft."

Pick up your bible and get some powerful scriptures that will be a sword in your hand. Then you can tell them what the Word of God says and that will be way more effective than any ideas you can come up with.

You can say, "I sense that you are bitter." They may receive that. However, if you say, *"…and though I give my body to be burned, but have not love, it profits me nothing."* This is going to be more effective. (1 Corinthians 13:3)

Perhaps you have someone that is loaded with bitterness and not only can you see it, but everyone else can too. If they cannot see it, how can you address them? You can address them using the Word of God.

You can say, "You think you are so righteous. Your flesh stinks. There is nothing good in it. You think you are not bitter. However, according to the Word of God, the only thing good in you is Jesus Christ and Him glorified.

Do not think that you have anything to offer God. You can give your body to be burned, you can give away to charity and you can even do good works. However, without the agape love of Christ, you are nothing."

 Chisel using the Word, not your own ideas.

The Word of God is a sword - use it. Do not stand there slapping them around in your own strength because that Word also applies to you too. There is nothing good in you either. You are not the standard. The Word of God is the standard.

Whether you are addressing a root of temporal values, a spirit of lust, a root of bitterness, a need for acceptance or a need for recognition, you need to go to the Word and get your answers from the Word and apply it. Only then will you see change.

## 3. Stand in the Anointing

Also, use the anointing. Do not pick up ten scriptures to back up what you are saying. That is not what I am talking about. I can go to someone and say, "This is what the Scriptures say on bitterness..."

When I say it like that, who cares? However, when I look at them and say, "This scripture says rebellion is as the sin of witchcraft. You are in rebellion and therefore you are in witchcraft right now and that is unacceptable according to the Word."

I could sit and teach you about rebellion and bitterness and I could give you all the scriptures and a very sound teaching. You would sit there and think, "That is very interesting."

However, if I apply the scripture to you, it is different. I can say, "Do you know that rebellion is as the sin of witchcraft? It is not a bad habit, a template from the past or a hurt that you got twenty years ago. It is witchcraft. It is sin. It is unacceptable.

You are walking in the flesh, which is a position and state that is unacceptable to God. If you want God to use you and if you want to rise up in His anointing, then you better deal with this sin in your life now."

That means applying the Word. Do not hit them with ten scriptures back to back please. All they are going to do with all those scriptures is skim them. However, if you take the Word and directly apply it to them under the anointing, they will be looking up the reference.

Then later on, when it is their turn to work with someone that is doing the same thing, they will be using the same scripture.

You see, it is not good enough for me to sit here and apply the Word with my head. I applied those scriptures to you using a conviction anointing. When someone is flowing in that anointing, the first thing you will say is, "Is that me?"

You cannot help but feel that it applies to you in some way. You feel the Word coming into your heart and challenging you. Whether you are actually in rebellion or not, you just want to say, "Lord, I give it up the flesh - just in case I am in rebellion."

 Stand in faith to chisel under the anointing.

When you apply the anointing, it adds such a power to the Word because it is not simply a logos word anymore. It becomes a rhema word. How do you apply the anointing? You apply it by faith.

Depending on which office you are in, you can tap into your spirit at any time and tap into the anointing. The Scriptures say that the gifts and callings of God are irrevocable. You have it in you at all times.

If you flow in the prophetic gifts, then you can tap into them at any time. When you are speaking to your disciple and you are applying a scripture, tap into your spirit. If it helps, pretend that you are standing behind the pulpit.

Pretend that you are speaking to a crowd. Pretend that the Lord Jesus is right there speaking to them through you. Picture yourself standing in the glory cloud. Close your eyes and picture the anointing on you. Do whatever it takes to tap into your spirit.

## "Trigger" the Anointing

The best way to tap into that anointing is to remember a time when you felt it strongly. Think about a time when God used you and you felt that conviction anointing. Go back to that time in your mind and remember how it felt and tap into that.

Sometimes that memory alone can trigger those emotions and cause the anointing to flow out of you, because you have built a template for it. You have built a template for the gifts. The first time you received them and used them, you built a good template.

You can tap into those templates. We do this with music all the time. Think about a song that you would deem "anointed." Each time it is played you always feel the anointing. Why? It is because you created a template with that song or circumstance.

I remember I received a breakthrough with this. When I was going through my training, the Lord challenged me and said, "How can you stand behind the pulpit and be so anointed, but in the social groups you have nothing to say and are so insecure?"

I said, "It is my point of weakness. I do not feel like a leader. I do not feel like I have anything to say."

He said, "You know what it is like behind the pulpit. Now, when you speak to people, just imagine that you are behind the pulpit. Put your strength into your place of weakness"

So I did just that. I imagined that I was behind the pulpit. I thought about what it felt like when I was behind the pulpit. I realized that when I am behind the pulpit, I do not care what anyone thinks. In this point of strength I was secure in myself and in what God had given me.

I did not flinch. I was not afraid to speak the Word, because it was not my word, it was His word. So why was I suddenly afraid when I was in a social setting? By tapping into my strength, the Word and the Lord, I was able to tap into my spirit and release the same anointing.

It got to the point where it was so comfortable that whether I was on or off the pulpit, I was the same person. It did not matter where I was.

Go back to when you did flow in the anointing. Go back to the time when you were walking in the spirit, not in the flesh and tap into that anointing. Remember how it felt. You will also remember that at that time there was a flow there that came up from within you.

If you were flowing in the external anointing, then there was a step of faith that you took. There is always something that you do or feel. Tap into that again, apply the Word and release that anointing as you speak.

Release it by faith. Ask the Holy Spirit to help you and He will. He will do it not for you, but for the person that is reaching out to the Lord saying, "Lord, I need this. I need help." Their faith will cause you to get the breakthrough that you need.

I wish that I could say that everyone you chisel will come back to you and say, "Thank you for that chisel. I was sitting here the whole week hoping for a chisel and here it is. It was an answer to my prayer to hear you chisel my most intimate weaknesses.

It was the best time that I had all week. In fact, I would rather have that chisel than to sit next to the pool on a nice summer's day."

Hardly! You should count yourself blessed if just one person comes back and says, "Thank you for all the time, blood, sweat and tears that you invested into that chisel for me."

## 4. Chisel with Intent

However, mostly you are going to get people spewing at you. They are going to do a number of things. If they are expressive and full of bitterness, then they will spew at you about everything that ever bugged them with every leader that they are bitter against.

If they do that, then it is a good sign because that is the intent of the chisel. The intent is to bring that out. They are going to spew everything at you that they were ever afraid to say to their mother, father or any of their leaders.

When they do that it is going to be full of filthy, rotten flesh. After a day or two when they cool down and you send that letter back to them saying, "Now, do you still want to tell me that you do not have any bitterness?"

 The point of a chisel is to get a reaction.

Those few words will be enough conviction for them. Let them react because they are supposed to react. That is the idea of the chisel. It hits the flaw and nobody likes it. So if you get such a reaction, then you have a very good disciple.

Their reaction shows that they are being open and honest with you. When you hit something they will show you that whatever you just hit – hurts! The kind of person that I love is the one that travails when I give them a chisel.

They travail and struggle and then they come back and say, "That hurt like nothing else. I know that you are right and I am prepared to see that you are right. However, everything in me wants to tell you to go where the sun does not shine."

I love and respect such a disciple because you can work with them. Then you can write back and say, "Can you see now that this is an area of weakness in your life? Can you see that satan has something to use against you?"

Then you can assist them through it. Yet, I cannot bear when someone says, "You are absolutely right! I see it now and I prayed about it last night. I gave it to the Lord and I feel that I got a breakthrough. Everything is good now. What do you want me to do next?"

## Do not Side Step

Do not do that! All you are doing is sidestepping the chisel. You are saying, "Ouch, that hurt. However, let me just tell the mentor something that will make them happy. This way they will leave that sore point alone and we do not have to look at it anymore."

The agreeable ones are the toughest to work with. I have never been the agreeable type of disciple that sits back and says, "You are right. That is wonderful." No. It is not wonderful. The chisel is never meant to be wonderful.

So do not look for or desire wonderful responses. Look for the responses of spewing, bitterness and flesh. That is what you want to see, because then you can deal with it. You cannot deal with it if they are hiding behind a mask.

## Don't Fear Failure

You have to be prepared to handle that kind of backlash, because it is coming. You have to be strong in yourself. You cannot sit there thinking that you missed it because you may have given a chisel in the flesh and failed.

It does not matter. If you are in this to truly pour out what you have and allow God to use you, then God will even use your mistakes. That is the grace of God. He has them on this train. He is just using you, even in your flesh sometimes.

Sometimes, when you are chiseling somebody, you have to feel your way around a bit. You may sense that something is wrong in the spirit, but they keep on doing this side stepping dance.

Every time you ask if there is a problem they just say, "No. There is no problem at all." So then you have to say, "Is it here? Is it there?" There will be times that you will hit wrongly. You will say, "Is your problem this?"

Then you will find out that there was no problem at all with the direction you chose. Yet, the point is that it will cause them to react and when they react you will see the problem right in front of you. It does not have to be the initial thing that you hit.

They may say, "The chisel is just so unfair and unjust." Exactly! Sometimes you are put in a situation where things are unjust, but when you are put in that situation, how will you respond?

> It is not what happens to you in Life – It is how you respond that defines you.

Their very response is what you are trying to pull out of them. How else will they know where their "sore points" are, unless you expose them? Sometimes, you will miss it completely. Yet, their response will show that you hit something. They will say, "You are wrong... "And then they will start spewing off.

You can say, "I may have been wrong, but did it justify your response? If satan comes along and uses someone to pull that string in you again, then what is going to come out?" Whether you are right or wrong is actually irrelevant.

Let me tell you that you will actually be wrong around fifty percent of the time, at the least. Yet, that is the idea. You are applying pressures to them in order to bring things out of them.

## God Will Use Injustice

God will use things that are unjust and unfair. Why? If someone walks up to me and says, "I love and appreciate you and you are wonderful," am I going to react negatively to that? No, I will say, "Thank you."

You are not going to see any flesh busting out there. However, if someone comes to me and insults me or says things that are unfair, now how am I going to react? God does not have time to arrange circumstances all the time for your disciple to experience and face this.

## When to Back Off

You will be the vessel that He will use to bring about something that is unfair. If they cannot take it from you, then they are going to have to get the test from the world. That is always my final warning that I give my disciples.

I say, "Look, if you do not take this chisel from me right now, then God is going to use somebody else." If they do not take the chisel from you, then stop chiseling. If they insist on skipping through and spewing but not getting a conviction, then back off entirely.

Stop talking and stop writing. You must now wait and allow the Holy Spirit to take over and arrange circumstances because you did what you could do and had to do. Yet, you keep thinking that you are responsible and you keep on pushing.

Do not push. Stop and back off. Allow the Holy Spirit to do it because in just a short time, they will come back to you telling you how they hit a wall and how much everything went wrong.

Then you can say, "Is that right? Are you ready to listen now? Are you really ready to receive the truth?" By then, they are usually ready to receive the truth. The Lord will try to use you first because it will make their training go quicker and it will be more effective.

Do not be afraid to be the chisel. It is one of the most powerful tools in mentorship or training.

## 5. Identify the Root

Identify the root problems in your disciple's response. To see the root of their problems, is very difficult, when somebody comes back spewing at you and exposing your failures,

They will say, "Who do you think you are? I know that you failed here and there. I know what you said to your other disciples as well. How can you come and tell me this, when I know that your life does not line up?"

You have to look past that. Do not jump and start justifying yourself. It is not about you. Do not ever respond to a backlash with justification because God is your justification and vindicator.

Do not say, "I just want you to understand where I am coming from." I do not care where you are coming from. Where is the Word of God coming from? Do not justify yourself. Cut past the junk and get to the root.

There are three main roots of the flesh. They are bitterness, lust and temporal values. You are bound to find at least one of them.

 **Tools of the Trade**

I want to give you a quick list in the order of chiseling and then I am going to give you a quick interlude of the differences between them.

## The Order for Chiseling

**Step 1:** Chisel

**Step 2:** Identify the Root Problem

**Step 3:** Bring Healing

**Step 4:** Give an Impartation

We are going to cover healing and impartation in the next chapter. Chisel them, but do not leave it there – follow through. You need to identify the root problem and what God is exposing in them.

It depends on the vein that you are mentoring in. Then after you have identified the problem, heal and lastly impart the new thing to them that will replace the old. Let us have a quick look at correction vs. chiseling and advice vs. direct orders.

## Correction

What is the difference between correction and chiseling? I may tell someone that they are out of line and then they will say, "Colette gave me such a chisel."

I am thinking, "I told her not to over pack the dishwasher. That is a chisel?"

Some people have the idea that if you just look at someone sideways, that you are giving them a chisel.

"My husband told me to put his socks in the drawer. Wow, he really chiseled me there!"

What are you talking about? All you received was a correction. What is the difference? Let me explain that difference to you.

## 1. From Authority to Subordinate

Firstly, a correction is given from an authority figure to a subordinate.

Whether a correction is based on the Word regarding your spiritual life or it is of an administrative nature, it is given from someone over you.

You can correct someone using the Scriptures as well. If you see a brother having an affair or in some way getting into sin, even though you are not above them, the Word of God is and you have every right as a believer to say, "That is sin according to the Word of God."

In fact, what do the Scriptures say to do if your brother sins against you? You are to go to your brother and correct him. If he has sinned according to the Word, then you have every right to correct him because the Word is the authority.

If someone sins against the Word, then you have every right as a believer to say, "That does not line up with the Word of God." Of course, you do not go around correcting everyone.

However, a correction is generally given from an authority to a subordinate - whether it is an apostle or a pastor above you, your husband, your boss or even a mother (if you are a natural or spiritual child).

## 2. Based on a Realm of Administration.

If you are a parent, it is assumed that you correct your children all the time. You do not say that you really had to chisel your child about leaving their clothes on the floor. That is not a chisel - it is a simple correction.

Correction is given out of administration. When I mess something up in my realm, I receive a correction in accordance to my responsibilities.

Let us say for example that I asked one of my team to give me a list of all the fivefold ministry school students and their trainers by Monday first thing in the morning. If they do not submit the list or they submit it incorrectly, then I am going to go to them and say, "What is this?"

If they say, "I messed up," I am then going to let them know that it is unacceptable. I am going to say, "If I ask you for a list, then get me the list. It needs to be here on time. Why is it not on time?"

Am I chiseling them here? No, I am correcting them because it is in the realm of administration. That was their realm of responsibility and they failed in that realm of responsibility.

## 3. Addresses Mistakes and Failures

A correction deals with mistakes and failures. It is not about chiseling off the flesh. It does not have a deep and spiritual meaning. You just made a mistake or failed in some way in your responsibilities that are in your realm and so you get a correction for it.

If my daughter leaves her clothes on the floor after I have told her many times to put them away, then she is going to get a correction. If I say to my children, "Do not go outside," but they go outside anyway, then they are going to get a correction.

These things are all corrections, not chisels.

## Chiseling

What is chiseling? Firstly, chiseling is something given only from a mentor to a disciple. Why? It is because it is a process of training that is meant to bring out weaknesses and impart strengths.

If you are chiseling a person, then you want a reaction from them. However, if I give one of my team an order, then I desire obedience from them. I do not want them to say, "I had a bad template that was triggered and I have bitterness towards someone. That is why I stayed in bed all day instead of doing the job."

I do not care. I just wanted the report on my desk by the morning. I am only giving a correction. On the other hand, a mentor gives a chisel to get a reaction and pull something out. They want the tears and the flesh, so that they can deal with the deeper issues.

They want to see change in the person. They want to deal with things like character traits. You want to challenge temperamental weaknesses and strengths. You are going to go into the deepest spiritual issues.

## 1. Only Mentors Chisel

A mentor is the only one that should be chiseling anybody. If you do not have a disciple, then you should not be going around chiseling anyone. If you are not a mentor, then what are you doing going around chiseling people for?

If you are in a position of leadership, then by all means you are more than welcome to correct those that have failed under your authority. Correction and discipline is in God's order.

However, if you are going to chisel someone to shape, mold and change them, then they better have submitted to you first. Even as a pastor, you have no right, to go around chiseling, shaping and molding people's lives without permission.

You can correct, but you have no right to chisel.

Now, if someone comes to me and asks, "When is something that a leader says advice and when is it a direct order?"

## 2. Advice is Optional

If they say, "I have this idea. My husband and I would like to do this. What do you think?" Whatever I share after that is advice. It relates to everything outside of the mentorship realm.

## Counsel Shared Outside of the Mentorship Realm

If you are training someone in the prophetic, anything that does not pertain to the prophetic is outside of the mentorship realm and they do not have to disclose it to you.

If they want to have babies, go on vacation, move houses or even change jobs, then it has nothing to do with you whatsoever because those things fall outside of the mentorship realm. Whatever you say about these things is simply advice.

They can choose to take your advice, but they have no obligation to listen to you at all. This is simply advice given naturalistically and through personal experience and wisdom. In other words, it is your personal opinion. You can say, "This is what I think, but you do not have to take it."

Even Apostle Paul said, "If someone is single, then I think that they should remain single, but that is just my opinion and my choice. It is not what God is saying, it is what I am saying." (1 Cor 7:6)

## Direct Orders

What is a direct order? A direct order is something given in context to your training and it is never asked for, but rather offered. It is based on the Word, not your personal opinion, and it is given with revelation and spiritual wisdom.

### Given in Context of Training

A direct order is given in context of the training. Again, you cannot tell a person what job they can or cannot have, you cannot tell someone how to take care of their wife, what to do with their business, how many children they can have or where to work.

You should only be giving orders in relation to the training that they are in. You have no business dealing with their personal lives. You do not even have a say in what church they go to, unless it relates to the training specifically.

You may only challenge and give direct orders according to the training.

---

 **Tools of the Trade**

---

In conclusion, I want to summarize those four steps that you need to follow.

1. When giving a chisel, you chisel hard.

2. After chiseling them, you need to identify the root.

3. Once you have identified the root of the flesh or the flaw in them, you must then bring healing.

4. Finally, give an impartation, so that they can rise up to be the leader that you are.

# CHAPTER 12:
# Healing, Impartation & Breaking Ties

## Gifts are Meant to be Special

During Christmas time, although there is a lot of commercialism around, there is still something about getting a special gift from a special someone as a surprise.

When you see that brightly wrapped package with a ribbon on it, you know it is a good thing and you get excited about it. You might not know what is inside, but you somehow know that it will be something that will bless you.

You have an idea that it is something that will be a joy to you. Now, we all know that not all the gifts that we receive are blessings. Sometimes people give you gifts that they really wanted, because they do not know what you like.

Generally though, the concept of a gift is that you receive something that is just for you. It is something special where for that moment in your life, it is really about you.

Don't you wish that we had birthdays every day of the year? As a child, I remember thinking that if I could have one wish, it would be that I have a birthday every day.

This way I would be able to get a present every day of the year. My parents would be pretty broke, wouldn't they? Too bad that is not the way it works. Actually, I think that not getting them so often is the reason why they are so special.

It is because you do not get them all the time that they mean so much to you. You only get them once a year. You have to age. You have to qualify by going through a whole cycle of life before you can get your hands on that gift.

If we received them every day, we would lose interest. There is something special about waiting and counting down the months, weeks and days. If you are a child then you probably count down the hours and minutes too.

In the spirit, there are so many gifts for us to receive, but as it is in the natural, it is not something that happens every single day. In 2 Timothy 1:6, Paul says to Timothy:

> *Therefore I remind you to stir up the gift of God which is in you through the laying on of my hands.*

There is a reason why God called them gifts. Just like that brightly colored wrapping, there is something special about them. You are increased and you receive something that you wanted and desired. You are excited about it.

You have counted down the months, weeks, days and minutes and you cannot wait to get your hands on it.

It is not something that happens every day. You must go through a cycle of life in order to get it.

Depending on which training you are going through, that cycle may vary from a few weeks, to seven months, to nine months or even to years. It depends on you and on your training. However, there is something special at the end of every cycle of your training.

 The point of this journey is to receive a gift at the end.

At the end, there is a big, brightly colored, wrapped box just for you. It is a gift. Training is not all about death. At the end of the road there is a special something that God is going to give you.

He is going to give it to you through your mentor. If you are the mentor, then you are the one that is going to be imparting it to your disciple.

In the last chapter we looked at chiseling, bringing people to death and challenging their sin. I am going to continue that subject a bit but now take you from that process to the end of your mentorship.

## The Best for Last

This is the best part as far as I am concerned, because this is the part where you really see the most change.

You continually push through with the person and even as a mentor, some days you think that they are never going to get it.

You think that you are wasting your time. It will seem like you are continually chiseling and challenging them about the same things. You get discouraged and think that they will never rise up. However, this phase is almost like the final stage of labor.

This is where they push through, start receiving the anointing and the gifts and start actively applying them to their lives. This is the best part, so hang in there. Something good will come of it.

## How to Deal With Blockages and Bondages

Last time I spoke about how you need to address issues in a person. I am going to go through a fairly quick process of the steps that you should be taking when dealing with blockages and bondages in a person.

Sometimes, you get it backwards and you cannot understand why you are not making progress. You say, "I have this disciple and he has been going through this same problem again and again."

It is obvious then that you never dealt with that problem correctly and that is why it continually keeps coming up. If you have dealt with something, then it is dealt with, under the blood and resolved.

However, if it keeps coming up again and again, then you never resolved it. You have to go back to the drawing board and say, "Where have I failed? Where in the process did I miss it?"

If you do this backwards or if you miss a step, then you are going to mess up the whole equation. It is like this in mathematics. There are steps that you have to follow, if you want the equation to equal the same amount on either side of the equal sign.

You cannot just miss a whole bunch of steps. You must go through it in such an order that it comes to a proper end. So, let me help you a bit.

## 1. Identify the Root Problem – Personal Sin

Here is an example: You have a disciple that writes this whole big story to you saying that they have lots of problems in their life. Perhaps they say that they have a curse and things keep getting stolen. Maybe, they keep getting into fights with their spouse all the time.

What is the first thing that you are going to say? I know what you are thinking. You are thinking of saying, "There is a curse in your life." Yes, there is, but do you know what the first thing you need to say is?

You need to say, "There is personal sin in your life because in order for a curse to be in your life, there has to be personal sin in your life first. If you are familiar with the teachings in *Strategies of War*, then you understand this concept. Unfortunately though, some people took the principles on identifying curses a bit too far!

They read the principles and quickly identified the curses in their lives. Then they started blaming them on everybody around them!

"I am under a curse because of my best friend, my mother or someone else."

They forgot the most important principle of all, which is: Satan cannot gain license except through your own sin.

Until you have addressed personal sin, you do not even have a foot in the door. It is so easy to look around and point fingers and see who you can blame.

Your disciple has more than likely been doing this their whole life. However, they cannot understand why they do not rise up in ministry or why their life continues to go around in circles.

## The Danger of a Victim Mentality

They say, "It is because 'this' pastor would not receive me. It is because 'that' mentor would not impart to me. It is because my mother treated me badly and my father rejected me."

In their minds, the whole world is out to get them. Their circumstances are bad because of "bad luck". They had a bad day because of terrible traffic. Sure, we can blame it on our circumstances and so many other things..

At the end of the day though, what is the root of all problems? The root is sin! Do you have a problem? Does your disciple have a problem? What is the reason for that problem? The reason is personal sin.

Now until you have addressed personal sin, you will not even have a foot in the door. You say, "I imparted, I prayed, we dealt with curses related to all types of things and people. I cannot understand why they still have this problem."

Did you address their personal sin? It does not matter what someone else did, their sin has opened the door. If they have issues, then sin has opened the door. If you have not addressed personal sin, then you have just wasted all the time that you have invested.

> *Romans 6:12 Therefore do not let sin reign in your mortal body, that you should obey it in its lusts.*
> *13 And do not present your members as instruments of unrighteousness to sin, but present yourselves to God as being alive from the dead, and your members as instruments of righteousness to God.*

That is where the chisel has to hit hard and continually because personal sin (the flesh) is the ultimate flaw. Every time you walk out of the spirit, you walk in the flesh and you give license to satan. When you sin, you give license to the enemy and also to your flesh to start obeying all your evil desires, as it says in the passage above.

You know it as well as I do, that if you give license to satan, then you can kiss your ministry goodbye. You cannot allow them that luxury as a mentor.

You need to smash the victim mentality that says, "I had a bad life. I was abused. My father was an alcoholic. My life was tough and therefore I am justified in being bitter."

They will say, "I have these curses because of what everybody else did to me." People have gone through harder things in life and reacted differently. You can take two similar people and put them through the exact same circumstances in life and each one will respond differently.

One will respond well and come out of the whole situation fairly unscathed. The other one will be devastated and their whole life will fall apart. What makes the difference? What happened to them?

### It is Not What Happens to You in Life...

It is not what happened to them that makes the difference. It is how they responded to what happened to them. That is called personal sin. You will find all their templates and hurts from the past mixed in there too.

However, what do you usually find in each of those templates? You find sin. If your disciple comes to you and you can clearly identify a trigger, what are you going to say? You will say, "This is a trigger to a template of something that happened to you in the past."

Wrong. That's not what you should say. Instead you should say, "This is a trigger to a template from something that you responded to negatively in the past. It is not about what happened to you, it is about how you responded."

 Identify sin by addressing how they responded to life – Not what life did to them.

Until you deal with the personal sin and their wrong responses to life, they are not going to get a breakthrough. This is where the chisel has got to hit continuously. If you have not learned to hit on that flaw, then the next steps will be invalid.

Then it will be like trying to build on a foundation that is not there. Until they get a conviction of sin, they won't receive inner healing, they won't be able to deal with the demonic bondages and as a result you will experience a backlash.

Furthermore, they will not receive anything new from you either. It is tough because you feel sorry and bad for people. Unfortunately, you are not allowed that weakness as a mentor.

## 2. Make Them Take Responsibility

Once you have chiseled and brought them to death, then you can do inner healing and tell them that you understand. You need the balance of the two. There is a time to wield the chisel and there is a time to bring the oil.

However, I am afraid to tell you that the chisel comes first. It has to come first because they have to be brought to the cross. They have to be brought to a conviction and realize that the reason they are a failure in life is because of themselves and not someone else.

It is not even because of where they live, where they work or who they are. They are a failure because of themselves. They have not risen up into office or progressed as they should because of their choices and their decisions.

Why? It is because God never imposes His will on anyone. Hopefully, I can impart this correct mindset to you, and help you with this challenge to see things as you should. I want you to take responsibility.

If you fail with your disciple, is it their fault? No. It is your fault. Have you failed with disciple after disciple? Are you saying that you have just had a bad bunch of disciples? No. Those disciples just had a bad mentor.

If they truly submitted themselves to you and they never got a breakthrough, do not blame them. They are sheep. If a sheep drowns in the river, does the shepherd say, "Stupid sheep?"

## It's Up to You

No. He says, "I should have watched that sheep. I should have led that sheep better." If a wolf comes and eats the sheep, does the shepherd say, "Have a good snack, wolf?"

No. The shepherd runs after the sheep. He leaves the ninety-nine for the one sheep. That is a good shepherd. That is a good mentor. You say, "It is not my fault that the sheep want to be stupid and open their heart to the wolf."

 A good mentor guards the sheep and takes responsibility for their lives.

You are responsible as a mentor. If they are failing, it is because you are failing. Your first failure was calling them to mentorship. Obviously, you were not led.

Secondly, you do not know what you are doing or you are not following these steps correctly. While you are busy addressing their personal sin, take a good look in the mirror and address some of yours too.

## Stuck in the Middle

This always works as a double chisel. The Lord always asks you to chisel someone that has the same problem you struggled with, just to make sure that you are nice and humble when you deliver it.

Get rid of the victim mentality that says, "We cannot help the way we are. We cannot help the way it is." You can help it. You have a will and a choice. We are not like animals that are born with instincts and forced to follow a specific pattern in life.

God gave man a free will. Until you are able to identify personal sin, you will not be able to identify the root. Sometimes you have to hit a bit of personal sin before you can see the root clearly.

As I shared with you in the previous chapters, address the personal sin and address it hard with the Word of God. As you are addressing the sin, you will clearly see what the root of their problem is.

You are only ready to look at their templates, when you have brought them to conviction.

If you address a template without dealing with their sin first, what you are saying is that their problem is in the past. This is not true because their problem is not in the past. Their problem is very much in the present because this is where it is manifesting.

Sure, the problem may have started back there, but that is not where their problem remained! Their problem is right here with you. They are rebelling against authority. They want to run away and hide from pressure.

The problem is not back there, the problem is in the "here and now." They are responding to you incorrectly right now. So you have to deal with those problems, right now.

Sometimes though you do not want to apply that pressure. Instead you give them a way to escape. You say, "The reason you are this way or the reason that you are insecure is because of what your mother did to you. She did not tell you who you were. She did not affirm you.

Your father did not give you recognition and that is why you are striving now. That is why you have a spirit of strife and vainglory now. It is why you are pushing everyone down, backbiting and destroying people's lives. I understand."

No. I do not understand sin because the Father does not understand sin. If you want proof of that, take a look at the life of Christ to see how well the Father understood sin. When Christ got on the cross and took on the sins of the world, the Father crucified sin, until every drop of blood was drained from His body.

## Conviction of Present Day Sin

That is what the Father thinks of sin. Until you can bring them to conviction of their present day sin, then you cannot go back and deal with the template of the past. However, when you have the same failure in your life, you are too afraid to confront.

Because you have the same sin, you think, "If I confront them on their sin, what example am I?" Plus, you just do not want to look at your sin in the first place. So you say, "My problem is because of a template from the past and theirs is too."

You skip the sin and go straight to the template and then cannot understand why you are not getting the victory. You have not followed the process through correctly. You have not confronted their sin as it stands today.

When they have received a conviction and go to the Lord and say, "I have really messed up, please forgive me." Then you can say, "I believe the reason this is so hard for you to overcome is because of this template in the past that predisposes you to this sin."

## 3. Identify the Template

We have a will. We can decide not to listen to that sin. Yet, the templates of our past predispose us to it and make it so much easier to sin. It is not the template's fault that you are sinning. You chose to sin. However, the template makes it easier to sin.

Once they have received the conviction and they have cleansed their heart before God, then you can say, "Now we can deal with the template that is making it so easy for you to fall into this trap." Now is the time to step in and help them understand.

Now, you can address it and go back to what happened to them and deal with the emotions.

I am not going to labor this point here, because I cover it in a lot of detail in the Bonus Chapter on *Templates and Triggers.* Once you have looked at your disciple's personal sin, you will be able to sort through their feelings and identify what emotions were triggered inside of them.

It will vary according to person and circumstance, but the best place to start would be to look for an outburst of emotion that they were not able to control.

Perhaps something caused a sudden outburst of anger or fear. Although the anger seems to be the loudest emotion, you will need to look deeper at what triggered that anger. Go back to the template of the past and when you do, you will see a hurt, difficult circumstance and along with it a demonic bondage that was given license through their sin.

## 4. Dealing With the Demonic Bondage

> *Ephesians 4:26 "Be angry, and do not sin": do not let the sun go down on your wrath,*
> *27 nor give place to the devil.*

Never forget that when you open your heart to sin, by reacting to a situation in the flesh, that you give satan a foothold.

This is so important and it is another step that people either jump straight to or miss entirely. Once you have identified the template, you have to deal with the demonic bondage.

You must deal with that because whenever that person sins and triggers that template, that demonic bondage is triggered as well.

Your disciple can be going about their life and end up in a conflict or something. Suddenly, out of nowhere they respond in a strange way and you think, "Who is this person?"

You start seeing curses manifest in their life and you even feel oppression on them that you never felt before. You think, "Did I miss it? I have never felt this oppression on them before. Why am I feeling it now?"

It is because that template from the past has been stirred up. When they sinned again, they gave root to that demon again. The same demon they gave license to so long ago. So it is very important to identify the demonic bondage after you have identified the template.

Then make sure they pray it through and tell that thing to leave. They need to take away its license. I am not going to go through tons of scriptures and principles here, because these things are covered in *Strategies of War* and in the Bonus Chapter on *Templates and Triggers* at the end of this book.

If your disciple comes to you and says, "Everything was fine one minute and the next I was fighting with my husband and my kids started fighting with one another." Then you can clearly see that there is a spirit of strife.

Next, things get stolen and fear attacks them. These are clear signs of a curse. What are you going to say?

"It is a template from the past."

Wrong.

"It is a generational curse."

Wrong.

You need to look for personal sin. Once they have a conviction of their personal sin, then you can go back and look for templates and deal with the demonic bondage. Once you have done that, then they can truly be set free.

You can apply James 4:7 anytime.

> *"Therefore submit to God. Resist the devil and he will flee from you"*

What you need to remember when working with your disciple is that they gave license to satan and they need to take it away. It is important that they follow the process through.

## People Like Their Sin

Do not "gang up" on the demon and think that you can cast it out. They have authority. That is why conviction must come first. If they do not even have a conviction of their sin, then how can they possibly have a conviction to tell the demon to go?

You would think that when people have a demon that they would be quick to let it go. Do not fool yourself. Conviction of sin must come first, not conviction of a demon. People do not care if they have demons.

They may be terrified, but they do not care because they love their sin. Do not be deluded and think that if you tell somebody that they are demonized that they will be quick to let the demon go.

No. They are not going to want to let it go, because that demon allows them to hang onto their sin. That demon gives them an excuse to be the way they are and to make everyone accept them the way they are.

They are not convicted about that demon. They know that it is wrong, but until you bring a conviction of sin that demon is staying right there and it is not going anywhere. They can even pray and tell the demon to go and it will not because they are not convinced.

> Never forget – demons gain license through sin.

How many times have you prayed with someone and rebuked a demon and told it to go and the next time you saw that person, they still had that exact same demon?

Why did that happen? It happened because you failed to bring a conviction of sin. They are not convicted of their sin. They are not convicted that the demon should go because they want to hold onto their sin and that sin continues to give that demon license.

If you want to understand more about dealing with demons in ministry, then I recommend The *Prophetic Warrior* and *The Minister's Handbook* (Both published by Apostolic Movement International)

## Once They are Delivered

Even though you dealt with the demon, they are still not whole. You have gone and performed a surgery and you have dug out that root that is causing them to be sick, but it is not enough. When a surgeon cuts something out, he does not just cut it out and walk out of the operating room and says, "Have a nice day."

He takes the time to stitch them up with a surgical needle and to make sure everything is neat. He puts on antiseptic, wraps them up and leaves them in the hospital for a while, until they are healed. That is what we will look at in the next chapter.

**Tools of the Trade**

Let's take a look at what you have learned so far.

1. Identify personal sin

2. Make your disciple responsible for their life and actions

3. Once conviction comes, identify the template or hurt of the past

4. Identify the demonic bondage that was given license through that sin

5. Now we move on to the healing process

# CHAPTER 13:
# The Healing Process

Once the sin has been addressed and the template from the past exposed, the process of healing needs to take place next.

We have something that the worldly doctors do not have. We have the gift of healing available to us. After we have dealt with templates and demonic bondages, we can lay our hands on the person and speak healing to the memories of the past.

You have dealt with their response and the license that has been given to the enemy, but underneath all of that, there is still something that remains because something very hurtful occurred.

 Without ministering healing, your job is incomplete.

You must finish the process with healing because without the healing process, you leave the wound open to infection once again.

Have you encountered this case scenario? You minister to someone who gets victory in a specific area. They deal with their bitterness and other issues and even have a tremendous breakthrough in their circumstances.

Unfortunately though, a couple of months later, they seem to slip back into it bit by bit again. What happened? You more than likely did not apply inner healing.

They need healing because the pain is still there and the flesh is still responding negatively to that pain. When someone triggers that pain, they find themselves responding sinfully and giving satan license all over again.

Now, you are back to square one again. Healing must come, so that the pain is gone and they do not have to respond to it anymore. You are not getting victory because you are not following through with all of the steps.

## Receive the Impartation as You Read

Through all these things, there are so many principles to remember that you might not know where to start. I always tell everyone when going through these principles that they must get revelation.

I want you to read this book over and over again, until the principles sink deep within your spirit and when they are deep within your spirit, then forget everything that I have told you.

When you minister to your disciple, forget everything that I told you. What is in your spirit will come out. I am imparting to you right now. I am imparting the anointing, the wisdom and knowledge.

If you think that you can take these principles and apply them through head knowledge alone, then you will fail gloriously. You cannot remember all these things and know exactly how to go about them.

You need revelation from the Holy Spirit. When you let go and allow the Holy Spirit to lead you, you will hear my words reminding you of what to do. You will hear my words coming out of your spirit.

Yet, without the power of the Spirit and without getting revelation to tap into what is within you, you will not be a good mentor at all.

> Once you have studied all the principles, forget about them and let the Spirit give you wisdom.

## Inner Healing

So how do you go about ministering inner healing? Perhaps you think, "I do not flow in the gift of healing, so how do I pray for inner healing?" You are wondering if you have an ability to do that or not.

James 5:15-16 says,

*And the prayer of faith will save the sick, and the
Lord will raise him up. And if he has committed sins,
he will be forgiven.*
*16 Confess your trespasses to one another, and pray
for one another, that you may be healed. The
effective, fervent prayer of a righteous man avails
much.*

Are you a righteous man? If you are a believer, then
you are a righteous man. That means that if you pray
in faith, they will be healed. I just love the order of this
passage. It shows that only after sins have been
forgiven, can you pray for one another.

Confess your faults first and then pray for one
another. Do not just jump in and lay hands and pray. If
you are born again and you have faith, then you can
pray for inner healing.

This is not a gift that only the fivefold ministry
operates in. This is a gift that every believer can have,
if they have faith. It is the same with prophetic
ministry. Every believer can prophesy if they want to.

Every believer can speak in tongues and preach if they
want to. These are not gifts for specific offices. Sure,
some offices are stronger in specific gifts or have
more authority when using certain gifts, like when the
prophet speaks a decree.

However, you have the right to lay hands on
whomever you are praying with and to speak healing
to their emotional hurts by faith. If they have faith,

they will pull it out of you. I encourage you to grab hold of that faith.

Whether the sickness is physical, spiritual or mental, it does not matter. You have the ability to pray.

Now, they are headed for a breakthrough. You have dealt with the sin, bondages and even brought healing. Yet, there is still one last step that needs to be taken for them to really rise up.

Foot Note: The Subject of Inner Healing is something we have taught on a lot in other books. Look up *The Minister's Handbook*.

## Impartation

You have now removed the problems and veils that I spoke about previously that have prevented your disciple from receiving the anointing and rising up into their ministry. Through this process you have taken away one of the stumbling blocks.

Now that this stumbling block has been removed, they need to receive something from you. Depending on who you are and what your offices are, you will impart and give them the gifts in different ways.

Now that they have dealt with the stumbling block, they are ready to receive their reward. They get the nicely wrapped parcel that I spoke about in the last chapter. If they admire you, then often just by removing the blockages, they automatically receive the gifts you have.

They will automatically start to flow in the same anointing as you. The best way to impart without the "laying on of hands" is to include your disciple in what you are doing.

## Impartation Through "Hands On" Training

If you are a pastor and you're mentoring another pastor, include them in your work, ministry and counseling sessions. That alone will predispose them to the anointing and that will be enough for them to receive the gifts.

When you remove all those obstacles, the impartation will be instant. Unfortunately, many leaders leave this important part out. You have now done everything that you are supposed to do, but have you done the "hands-on" training?

It is not good enough to only teach someone something, but you also need to sit them down and teach them how to do it practically. If you are teaching someone to play a guitar, you should say, "No. You did that wrong. Try this."

That process is the most important. This is when the person learns the most. Are you doing that with your disciple? When last did you sit with your disciple and say, "This is how you prepare a sermon?"

 Hands-on training seals impartation.

Practical application is needed at the end. This is what seals the impartation and what puts everything together.

To see yourself walking out what your mentor has taught you brings the clarity that you needed. You suddenly realize that you are a pastor, prophet, teacher or whatever.

Unfortunately, throughout mentorship there is a lot of death for your disciple to go through. However, if they push through, at the end they will receive an impartation.

## Impartation Through Decree and Prophecy

If you are a prophet, you will take it one step further and you will decree the gifts of the Spirit over a person. It is very likely that they will even flow in the gifts the same way that you do. I have done this many times myself.

I have had times when I have released a decree over a crowd at a conference and whoever wanted the impartation, took it. Those that received the impartation suddenly began to flow in various gifts.

No matter what your ministry call is, you have the ability to speak forth the gifts into someone's life and to pray that the Holy Spirit takes the anointing that you have and give it to them. As you do this, the Holy Spirit may give you a prophetic word or a revelation to speak out.

This is certainly what happened with Elijah and Elisha. Elijah did not lay hands on Elisha. He shared a revelation instead which was that if Elisha stuck to him and saw him leave, the Lord would give him the mantle! (2 Kings 2)

 Impartation is the capstone of your mentorship relationship.

## Apostolic Impartation

Keep in mind that if you are an apostle, out of all the fivefold ministries, you are the one that can impart by the laying on of hands. You will impart what is in your spirit into theirs. When the apostle does this, it is by far the most powerful and strongest impartation. (Rom 1:11, 1 Thess 2:8)

It is the most powerful because they are not only receiving the gifts, but they are also receiving the anointing, the mandate and the operation of the gifts from you as an apostle. They will start to experience or sense the gift just like you do.

I noticed this when I started imparting to people. Suddenly, people would flow in the gifts in the same way that I did. They would see visions just as I did, simply because I imparted to them.

It is instant. However, the impartation cannot take place until they have dealt with all the obstacles that are preventing them from receiving in the spirit.

Yet, do not get discouraged when you have worked so hard with a person and you have pushed through and travailed. Then at the end, it seems that nothing comes of it. They may be going through prophetic training and cannot even prophesy.

I have a question for you. Did you teach them? Did you impart that wisdom to them? Did you take time to hear them prophesy and then say, "Try this or try that?" Have you assessed how they are doing?

Sometimes, we get too spiritual to assess the last practical phase. As they imitate you and as you give them the opportunity to imitate you, they will receive what you have, whether it is good or bad.

## Saying Goodbye

Then there comes the final step - saying goodbye. You want to hope that by this stage you have imparted, chiseled and healed all that you can. By this stage, you are hoping that you have done the right job.

I experienced this on a very naturalistic level when I looked at my daughters and how they were growing up. I could see that their dependency on Mommy was not as strong anymore.

In fact, when Mommy and Daddy disagreed about something, they were taking Daddy's side. The time had come... they had moved on from wanting Mommy all the time, to wanting Daddy.

There was this terrible feeling I had inside that my time with them was up. They were growing up now and there was this thought of, "Did I do it right? Did I teach and show them enough? Did I spend enough time with them and did I give them enough acceptance? Did I show them who they are in the Lord?"

All the principles go through your head during this phase and you wonder if you did everything right. Every single mentor will wonder if they did a good job. Yet, only once you have broken the ties and let them go will you know how you did.

I will only know if I have done a good job with my children after they leave home. After they receive from their Dad and then grow up and get married, I will see if I did a good job.

It is difficult to see in the process, because they are still changing and forming. However, a time will come when they will leave home and start doing and applying what they learned at home.

## When You Will See the Fruit

When they go and start their own homes is when I will be able to see if I have laid down the law correctly and put a good foundation into them. It is the same for you as a mentor.

Colette Toach

You keep on hanging on and thinking that there is one more thing that you have to tell them. You might think, there is one more thing that they need and just one more thing that you need to explain.

You are hoping that you did not leave anything out. You start cramming them with information, like before an exam. You give them as much as you can. Yet, there comes a time when you have to let go and realize that it is over.

The time has come. The phase of mentorship is over. The Holy Spirit has brought it to an end and it is time to let them go. If you do not let them go, they are not going to rise up.

# CHAPTER 14:
# Breaking the Mentorship Ties

I have received letters from people saying, "I have had this disciple now for the last twenty years or I have had this mentor for the last eight years." I think, "No wonder you have not grown or changed."

The changes and the growth only come after the break in mentorship. During the mentorship, you are constantly taking. It is only after the ties have been broken that you can go and apply everything.

If you cannot understand why your disciples are never rising up, it could be because you have not let them go and given them an opportunity to learn what you have poured into them? Even worse, you could have let them go and found out that you made a mess.

The great thing about mentorship is that you can have many of them. The Scripture says that you can have many instructors. You can be mentored time and time again. That is not a problem.

### The Step by Step Process of Letting Go

How do you identify the signs of when they have reached the phase where it is time to break the link and let them go? I have a few pointers. Firstly, they reach the office that you are mentoring them into. That one is obvious.

## 1. They Reach their Ministry Office or Mentorship Goal

If you are mentoring them in the prophetic and they reach prophetic office, then you know that it is over. Once they have been placed into office, cut the ties and say goodbye.

However, it is not always that simple, is it? Sometimes, you work with someone who fails. Sometimes you are like Elijah and you have a Gehazi that does not make it through to the end. (2 Kings 5)

## 2. If They are a "Gehazi" and Hit a Plateau

How do you know when it is time to let that person go? When they hit a plateau, it is time. If you keep trying to bring them to a place of getting a conviction in some area and they do not get it, then it is time.

They will pretend that they got a conviction, but they will keep coming back to the same place over and over again and they never rise higher. They will be running so well then suddenly hit a wall and you just cannot get them to move past it.

They will have the same bitterness or issue again and again. You will notice that they should be in office already, but they are hitting the same plateau again and again. If that is happening with your disciple, then you need to deliver one final chisel.

Not all disciples "make it." Some hit a plateau.

You will have to say, "This is it. You either take it now or leave. This is your final test. If you do not pass this test, you will not make it into office. I am not prepared to keep following through with you because you should have been in office already."

There are many times that I have had to give that response to someone. I had to say, "Do you know that you should have been in office months ago? This means that you are not taking the pressures like you are supposed to. You have backed off somewhere and you have failed. You either come right or we break ties and move on."

Either they will come right or they will not. If they do that is great. Then, you can follow through and lead them into office. However, if a little ways down the road they hit the same stumbling block, break links and call it a day.

It is time to let go. Perhaps they are not ready or maybe you failed. It does not matter. The point is that you need to move on with your life and they need to move on with theirs. Both of you will get nowhere, if you continue with this relationship.

Let it go. In the future, God may give them a second opportunity to receive from you, but obviously they are not ready right now. They have a different road, so give them that time. Break the links and let them go.

## 3. God Might Need to Bring a Sword

If you do not recognize the time to end the mentorship, the Lord will step in and you will experience what happened to Paul and Barnabas. They got into a huge fight. If you do not break the links correctly, then that is exactly what will happen.

If you try to hang on, you will come to a huge conflict that is going to split you right down the middle. That is fine. That is what God intended. Break the ties and let them go. It is time.

## 4. They Have Reached Your Level

Another sign is that they have come to your level. They can preach like you. Whatever you are mentoring them in, they can do it just like you and say it just like you. There is nothing more in that area that you have to give them.

It is now time to break links and to either let them go on and receive from someone else or start training them in a different area. Identify the signs and do not be afraid to let them go.

 Your job is done when your disciple matches you.

You will only know in time, if you did a good job or not. I know that this is probably a more difficult phase for the mentor than the disciple because you go through this travail of whether you did it right or not.

Also, you have developed such a relationship with this person that you want to keep being there for them. However, unless you let your natural children go, they can never rise up and start their own homes.

 **Tools of the Trade**

## Mentorship vs. Spiritual Parenting

It is the same with the spiritual as well. There has to come a time of letting go. Now, for the end, I want to take a quick look at the difference between mentorship and spiritual parenting.

I think most people confuse the two, which is why I spoke about what you should and should not be doing and what advice you should and should not be giving in the previous chapters. Never forget to stay focused on the area that you are mentoring in.

## Defining Mentorship

How is mentorship defined?

1. The mentor chooses the disciple.

2. You only deal with the subject at hand.

3. You must have a focused vision in mentorship.

4. You deal with one thing at a time and that is it.

5. Do not allow yourself to be distracted.

6. It is a temporary relationship.

7. When that person has received everything in that one realm, it is over.

8. You change the person by shaping them.

9. You apply the chisel to their lives.

10. They will become like you only in the area you mentored them in. (They will not be like you in their spiritual lives as a whole.)

They are like a piece of clay that you are continually molding, shaping, changing and applying things to. They imitate you, but it is not the main emphasis of the mentorship. The main emphasis comes through your application of pressure.

That is where most of the change comes. Yet, they will imitate you and be like you to a degree, but it is not the main emphasis of mentorship at all. The main emphasis is to have them stand up, do this, try this, listen to this and read that.

This is where the change comes in. The pressure you put on them shapes and changes them. The orders you give them, change them. They will imitate you because they admire you, but that is not the focus.

The focus is what you do to them and what you apply to their lives. They will become like you only in your area of expertise. Perhaps you have worked with someone and you are discouraged because they are not like you in many areas.

They are not meant to be like you in every area. They will only be like you in that one area. When you see them function in the area that you mentored them in, then you will see yourself.

If you mentored them in the prophetic, you will see that they flow exactly like you in prophetic ministry. However, when they stand up to teach, they will be nothing like you. In mentorship, you will only mentor in one area, so they will reflect you in that area only.

Have you not noticed that some people function so well in one area of ministry, but they are so bad in another? They probably had two different mentors. This is why they excel in one thing and are extremely terrible in the other.

It is because in mentorship you only see yourself in the specific area that you have mentored them in.

## Defining Spiritual Parenting

So, what does that leave for spiritual parenting?

**1.** The child chooses the parent.

The child looks up to and chooses the spiritual parent that they want to admire. In parenting, it affects every area of their life.

**2.** Every area of the person's life is affected – not just a singular aspect like in mentorship.

You will see the effects of spiritual parenting in the way a person walks, talks and operates in ministry. Even their natural lives are affected. How they bring up their children, how they speak to their spouses and how they handle life in general, will all be affected.

When someone receives spiritual parenting, they receive in more than one area. They receive something we call "spiritual DNA" from that parent.

**3.** This relationship is permanent, unless the person gives up that spiritual parent and moves to another one.

**4.** It is for the child to take from the parent.

The child is more active than the parent in this relationship. In mentorship, you are applying and giving instructions and orders. However, it is not the same in spiritual parenting. It is now reversed.

The child is the active one. If my children are hungry, I can hear it from the house next door. "Mommy, I am hungry! Feed me. I want food. I am thirsty. I am hot. I am tired." If you have been around growing children, you would have heard all of those things.

They will just rant on all day about everything. They are like birds that keep chirping with their mouths open. They want more and more. The mother bird is constantly running around to get them food.

That is what it is like in spiritual parenting. The child is on the heels of the parent, taking what they can. The parent is just the parent. The child takes all that they can. The child must ask for ministry or direction.

**5.** Leading by example is the primary function in spiritual parenting.

In mentorship, you are shaping, chiseling, applying, molding and dealing with one area. However, in parenting it is the other way around.

As the parent, you are more inactive, though not totally inactive. It is for the child to take, hunger, receive and run after you.

**6.** You will give more corrections than chisels.

If my child does something wrong, I do not chisel them. I correct them.

If my child fails or drops a glass, I do not chisel them. I say, "Next time, do not carry ten glasses." I correct them, because I have already laid down the law in their hearts. Hopefully, they have already been through a mentorship phase, so that only the correction is needed.

Spiritual parenting can only commence once mentorship is over.

You may have to give a chisel from time to time, but it is not the primary function, unless the parent is mentoring the child in something specific. That would be different.

If a parent sees potential in one of their spiritual children, they can say, "You really need to develop this particular area of your ministry." Then the chisels may come because mentorship is taking place in that one area.

Once they have reached the end, then that pressure will lift off again. However, generally, the parent will correct and not chisel. The parent will be available for the child to follow.

The parent will not sit there thinking up ways to try to get their message through to their kids. No. I don't do that with my kids. I let them live their lives and if I see something that needs to be addressed or if they need help, then I step in.

I prepare the food. Yet, if they have a need, they come to me. If a child falls and hurts itself they come to you and say, "Mommy, I am sore." Then you reach out and you heal them.

You do not sit there watching your child every minute of the day, to see if they fall, so that you can scoop them up. It does not work that way, but in mentorship it does.

In mentorship, that is exactly what you do, but not in spiritual parenting. Do not confuse the two. If you are mentoring someone, then you are mentoring someone. You cannot be a spiritual parent, until all mentorship ties are broken.

I want you to get a good picture of the two and then make sure you do not mix them up in your life. Make sure you do not parent your disciple. What happens in their personal life or even in the remaining areas of their spiritual life is none of your business.

Focus on the one thing that you are mentoring them into and then let them go. If God has raised you up as a spiritual parent, it will only come once the mentorship ties have been broken.

## Summary

Here is a quick summary of what we have discussed.

1.  Identify personal sin - You are never going to forget that one.

2.  Identify the templates

3.  Identify the demonic bondages

4.  Bring healing

5.  Impartation by examples of practical illustrations

6. Break links and let them go - when all is said and done and you have given all that you can, it is time to break the links and let them go.

Your job is now done. They will rise up and succeed and they will even be better than you. They will be more efficient than you and everyone will say, "Wow. What a great man or woman of God they are."

People may never know that you are the one that helped them to become that. That is the price of mentorship. You give everything that you are and have and then you step back and let them get the glory and surpass you.

 The prize of mentorship is to see your disciple outshine you.

It is about doing yourself out of a job and knowing that your reward is in the kingdom of God. You know that what you invested will remain. You have delivered fruit that will remain, whether you live or die.

Is that not why we are here? We should get to the place where our fruit remains. We should be remembered, not by our names or reputations, but by what we have imparted to others.

The life that we have given to others through our example and through our mentorship should remain.

# Templates
# and Triggers

# BONUS CHAPTER:
# Templates and Triggers

*1 Corinthians 9:22 "To the weak I became as weak, that I might win the weak. I have become all things to all men, that I might by all means save some.*
*23 Now this I do for the gospel's sake, that I may be partaker of it with you.*
*24 Do you not know that those who run in a race all run, but one receives the prize? Run in such a way that you may obtain it.*
*25 And everyone who competes for the prize is temperate in all things. Now they do it to obtain a perishable crown, but we for an imperishable crown."*

I was barely 13 years old (and quite a skinny, short, 13 year old at that). Our school had arranged a wilderness camp where we were all shipped out to the middle of nowhere and taught survival skills.

Well, I guess what survival meant to most of our leaders was a completely different concept to what I had in mind. My greatest challenge came the moment they handed us our rucksacks.

They had obviously got some old army rejects and on my little frame this thing was twice my size. By the time I had packed it full with all of my "necessities" I could hardly stand up – never mind go on a 5-mile hike!

I made the mistake that so many new campers always make. I packed it full of canned foods, drinks and books I thought I might need along the way. How heavy could one book be, right?

After a mile, I was out of breath. By the time we reached two I had blisters rising up out of my blisters. By the time the third mile was on the horizon I was happy to dump all my canned food and fast for the duration of our trip.

It is no surprise that even now years later, I still shudder at the thought of braving a hike or the "great outdoors." You now have a keen insight as to why my idea of a getaway is room service with a fully equipped bathroom, over a lumpy sleeping bag and a leaky tent!

I might have been just a naive 13 year old, but I wonder if you realize how fully packed your own spiritual backpack is right now.

You see the Lord has called us to run this race with all endurance and like me you are heading out on an adventure in which all the survival skills you have will count.

When it comes to the realm of leadership and your spiritual walk, you will learn, as I did, that carrying around unnecessary baggage only weighs you down.

> *"Hebrews 12:1 Therefore we also, since we are surrounded by so great a cloud of witnesses, let us lay aside every weight, and the sin which so easily*

*ensnares us, and let us run with endurance the race that is set before us,"*

## The Race You Have Run Up Until Now

You see, it has taken a lot of effort on your part to run this race up until now. Through all the principles you have learned along the way, you have pushed against the odds.

You have been like an athlete who has had his body pushed to the limit. You have stretched yourself and with the Lord's help, you have risen up.

Look at how far you have come! You have already accomplished so much. You have defied the odds and you have become stronger. Slowly you started to get the upper hand. Slowly you started to win this race.

But it does not come naturally, does it? Each time you press forward, it costs you. The ministry, the finances and the opportunities do not just fall into your lap.

You have to work hard for them. You have to exercise your faith, do spiritual warfare and stand on the Word daily. Yes, you are finally getting ahead in this race – but at what cost?

## What If I Had to Tell You That There Was an Easier Way?

What if I had to tell you that you could run this race in rest? How about if I said that you did not need to keep trying so hard all of the time?

How about if I told you that you could start to see more fruit in your life for less effort?

## Is There Really a Shortcut?

What you do not realize is that you have been trying to run this race with a very heavy weight on your back. While you are pushing forward all of the time, you start to take ground. However, if you stop for just a moment, it starts to weigh you down again.

Do you feel that you have to work hard to press forward with your ministry?

Do you feel that nothing comes easy to you?

The Word says that the Lord's yoke is easy and that His burden is light. This weight you feel is not of the Lord and I want to help set you free of it.

You do not need to carry this heavy rucksack around with you any longer! Step by step we are going to dig deep inside of it and pull out all those heavy weights that have been added to it.

### *There Is Good News...*

Do you know what the good news is? You have been pushing against so many odds for so long now, that once we lighten your load, you will fly!

All that faith and pushing through is going to pay off in a big way! So how about it? Ready to lighten that load and to put all these weights aside?

### Name That Weight

There is a reason why the writer of Hebrews says that we should lay aside every weight and then follows that statement with...and every sin that so easily besets us. You see, the secret lies in those few words.

Perhaps you have looked at the things that happened to you in the past as little hindrances. You look at the hurts and even your own anger and you tuck it back into the past, feeling like that is where they belong.

What you do not realize, child of God, is that you did not tuck them into the past. Instead you tucked them into your rucksack and now they are weighing you down.

You know when I was on that long hike, it did not matter if I looked at my rucksack or not. It did not matter if I believed the rucksack was there or not. My aching shoulders and back told me clearly that it was there.

It does not matter if you are afraid to look at the past or even at your failures. It does not matter if you refuse to delve into the things that you know you should. Just because you do not want to look at it, does not mean that it is not there.

Step by step, these things are weighing you down and what you need is a process of conviction, healing and victory!

Consider how you grew up. As a young child you probably did not know the Lord like you do now. You certainly did not have the firm scriptural foundation in your life that you have right now.

## One Thing That We All Have in Common

In fact, you knew very little about the world around you. And so each time you faced a difficult or painful situation, you would have reacted to that situation out of what was already inside of you.

Now tell me, what is the one thing that we are ALL born with? Regardless of whether we know Christ or not, every single human is born with one overpowering force that was given power when Adam said "yes" to Eve.

THE FLESH!

Without the knowledge of the Word and the Lord Jesus that you have now, I guarantee that most of the choices you made growing up were based on the flesh and not the Word.

Here is the problem though. Something quite incredible happened the very first time you made that choice.

## A Template is Formed

When a child faces a stressful situation for the very first time, how is that child likely to respond? Well, unless that child is Jesus Christ, they are likely to respond in the flesh.

The problem is though, that the moment they do that, they create a foundation for life. Every time they face that same event again in the future, before they can even think about it, the sinful response comes out.

Give that child another 20 or 30 years and you have an adult with some seriously messed up templates all based on a sinful reaction.

## Let's Make This Practical

Not sure if you understand me? Why don't we go to the beginning of your hike through life? Why don't we go back to the beginning and see what the Lord shows.

Can you remember your first day at school? Now for me, I had many such days. In fact, by the time I left high school, I had experienced 12 different school uniforms, "first days" and new starts.

I was small and insecure. I did not make friends easily, which made me a good target for other kids needing to prove something. I remember sitting in the classroom feeling as comfortable as a baby lamb in a lion exhibit at the zoo.

I remember what looked like one of the popular kids coming up and asking me questions about myself. I thought, "Hey this will not be so bad." So I opened up and shared.

That same person was the first to make fun of me and turn those things I said against me.

I can almost feel you squirming in your shoes. Now I might have been a Pastor's kid, but that does not mean I was walking in the spirit 24/7. No, my first response was anger, hurt and bitterness. Why shouldn't it be?

It was my parent's fault for making me go to another school. It was the kid's fault for making fun of me. The world was at fault and I reveled in it.

It is experiences such as these that formed a good and solid template. The template looked like this:

- Coming into a new situation and not being part of the status quo

- New school or environment

- Popular kids or "beautiful people" around me

### *My Response When Faced With These Circumstances?*

- Fear of rejection

- Insecurity

- Bitterness

- Shut myself off from everyone or try to perform

We grow up and notch experiences such as these down to, "that's just life." But is it? Are these experiences just normal phases of growing up?

They are if they do not leave hurts or scars. These can be overlooked if you reacted correctly to that situation.

I too covered this over and grew up in the Lord. I even started to rise up in ministry and manage to avoid getting myself into a situation like that again. You see, behind the pulpit, it was easy to have the upper hand.

The Lord would not leave it at that though. He had other plans. Being a good preacher was not good enough. I came to learn that to change lives, you need to get involved in people's lives. It meant getting off the pulpit and going to where the people were.

That meant putting myself in a position that mirrored the one I just described.

## 20 Years Later...

We had a seminar and I was comfortable behind the pulpit. However, as things worked out, we ended up doing a lot of social interaction with everyone afterwards. This became a trend in our ministry and one I now love.

I was hardly thrilled back then though. The moment I stepped into the room after the meeting, it was if a gun was triggered inside of me and I felt myself walking down an old road.

Without even trying, suddenly feelings of fear, insecurity and bitterness started to rise up.

WHAT WAS GOING ON?

I am meant to be ministering to these people, but all I wanted to do was run away.

The Lord had set the stage beautifully for me. He had arranged a set of circumstances that mirrored that childhood experience to a tee.

Without even trying, all those crazy emotions and irrational fears rose up out of me. I wanted to run out of the room and hide.

Fortunately for me though, I did have an upper hand this time. I had gone through some teachings and I knew what a trigger felt like when I had one.

- Emotions I could not explain

- Memories of the past suddenly coming up

- A desire to escape and react

I had some weights to pull out of my rucksack. Perhaps while I was behind the pulpit, I could get away with it, but now the race was on. Those weights that were hidden for so long were being exposed and they had to go.

I am sure that by now you realize that I am not just spilling my guts for your pure entertainment. I am getting to a point here.

That one silly template could seriously have hindered my ministry had I not dealt with it. If I had not dealt with it, it could very well have changed the entire course of what I am doing for God right now. I certainly would not be so closely involved with others.

I would not be a mentor or a spiritual parent. Most of all, I would never have gotten close enough to anyone to reach them for Jesus.

Child of God, the weights you are carrying around are more deadly than you realize. Not only are they weighing you down now, but they are also set to steal the blessing that God has in store for you.

So how about it? Ready to ditch those weights?

Oh yes, just in case you are wondering, I was able to deal with that template. I think the relationship I have with you is proof of that!

## What to Watch Out For

Identifying a trigger is probably the biggest step forward. I have found that even though I know the principles well, it still takes me a while to "get it."

That is why it helps if you have a team or a spouse that can help identify when you are not acting like yourself.

### Seeing It from the Outside

What I am going to give you here is a head's up. Imagine you are sitting across the way from me and I am handing out all my secrets on leadership.

No one knows you better than your spouse. Of course if you have spiritual parents or a mentor, then you will find that God will use them first to point things out to you.

Do not think that just because you know the principles that it is obvious. Very often you need someone from the outside to say, "Hey! Do you know you have a huge 'CRUCIFY ME!' Sticker on your back?"

If you are the spouse or mentor, you will notice that someone is triggering by identifying the points listed below. Mark these and keep them handy, because you will find yourself using them over and over again.

## 1. Extreme Changes in Emotion

When someone is triggering they will not be in control of their emotions. This might mean expressing loudly, or even clamming up.

## 2. Stories From the Past

I have found that when someone is triggering to something from the past, they suddenly start telling stories from that era. Now just because someone is telling an old story, it does not mean that they are triggering! However, if they start telling old stories out of nowhere, it can indicate that something from that era is being stirred up.

## 3. Reverting to Behavior from the Past

This is a very clear sign. If you have been working with someone for a very long time and suddenly they start acting childlike or reverting back to behavior from the past, the chances are, you are looking at a trigger.

## 4. Change in Language and Speech

In my personal experience, in working with folks whose first language is not English, when they trigger, they suddenly struggle to speak English! I know it sounds crazy, but look out for that one.

## 5. Unreasonable Behavior

Out of nowhere, that person begins to act strangely. Perhaps trying to relive events from the past or act in ways that they never have before.

## 6. Curses Manifesting

Now the thing is, when those templates are stirred up, so is the sin and the license the enemy was given! It is like that rucksack not only contains rocks, but sometimes snakes that lie hidden. You start shaking weights and the snakes will get uncomfortable and start crawling out.

Ok...I know it is not a pretty picture, but I think it illustrates my point. If there is a sudden onslaught of things being lost, broken or stolen and if you are fighting with everyone around you then there is a curse in the camp!

Add that to these other points and you can see a trigger loud and clear.

## Seeing it From Within

If you are the one triggering, these points apply to you as well. Look out for emotions that are raging out of control.

- Emotions out of control

- Memories from the past suddenly come to your mind

- You feel like rebelling or acting out, even though you know it is wrong.

## Dealing With It – Step by Step

Ok, there is no doubt about it – there is something that God is exposing. Something that happened to you in the past is causing some serious problems in your present. How do you deal with it?

Nope, I am certainly the lady of step 1…2…3… so I do not plan to disappoint you.

Like I said, identifying that you are triggering is your first big leap forward. Just by "seeing" it, you will immediately feel the emotions ebb.

So how about we move on to Step 1 shall we?

## Step 1: Identify It

Consider how you are feeling right now, and then ask yourself this question:

"When was the last time I felt this exact same way?"

Continue to ask yourself this question and trace back those memories until as far back as you can identify. This is where spiritual revelation really counts and why having a prophet around during a time like this is the best.

It is how we can function as a team. If you have a mentor, you are in a good place. Let your mentor walk through these memories with you. It is a lot easier than trying to do it alone.

Continue working through your memories until the earliest and most painful one sticks out to you.

You will usually identify the memory that 'started it all' because when you bring it back to your memory, you still feel the sting in it.

## Step 2: Change it!

Now identifying the original template is not enough. You responded badly back then. Ok, let's make it practical again.

Considering all I have taught so far, have any templates of the past come to your mind? Is there a situation that stands out to you particularly? Do you still feel the sting in that memory?

Now let me ask you, "How did you react to that situation?"

Rebellion? Anger? Fear? Jealousy?

You know your own heart and you know where the Lord is putting His finger. This feeling you have bottled up inside is the very thing that is keeping this template anchored in your life. Are you ready to let it go?

Then you begin by applying James 4:7. Submit yourself to the Lord and then you can deal with the enemy. Let your anger go. Repent of the sinful response.

This is the first stage. The second stage is to forgive the person that offended or hurt you.

The easiest way to do this is to see them through the Lord's eyes. Take yourself out of the situation and see things from their point of view.

This is very powerful! Give this a try right now. Bring up the memory that is bothering you. Now try to see this situation through the other person's eyes.

Let me use my own template as an illustration for you.

In my mind, I see those kids picking on me, laughing and making fun of my shabby clothes. Firstly, I let go of the bitterness and fear, because Jesus is standing right behind me. I am not alone anymore. He is right there and He is on my side!

I let go of my anger and I take His hand. Then I look at those kids and see something I did not before. They are caught in a system of their own. To stay popular, that kid always has to keep ahead of the pack. They have a continual expectation and striving in them to keep up with everyone else.

The others cannot reach out to me, because it would mean also being teased. They are not willing to pay that price. So they play along ignorantly. They do not know the Lord and they do not know any better. What kind of models have they had?

If I allow myself to be angry, I am no better than them. I see Jesus pick me up and carry me out of that situation. They stay limited in their thinking, but I can take this situation and use it to rise up.

Do you get the idea? Allow Jesus into your memory right now, and you will also begin to get the victory!

## Step 3: Kick the Devil Out!

So many people just want to blame the devil for everything and go right into warfare when things go wrong. No that is why James tells us to submit our hearts first. Deal with the beam in your own eye and you will have all the strength you need to deal with the enemy.

Once you have dealt with your own sin, only then are you ready to get rid of the enemy in your life.

He was only too happy to keep you angry and bitter. He was only too happy to help your fear along. He was also only too happy to encourage you to become strong and controlling, to prevent you from rising up.

However along with that has come a host of other things that are not a blessing! Now that you have dealt with your heart, stand up in boldness and tell the enemy to leave.

## Struggling with Generational Curses

What I am sharing here is the best way to deal with generational curses. Your sinful templates are what keep those generational curses securely in place.

Do you have any bitterness towards your parents? How about a sense of fear, obligation or jealousy? All of these things keep your templates anchored in your life and make your race hard to run.

It is time to lay aside the weights, child of God. It is time to not only run this race that is before you, but to win it!

## Seasons

You will find that the Lord will take you through seasons of dealing with sinful templates. It is a major part of prophetic training, but every leader will find the Lord dealing with things at one time or another.

I am pretty sure after reading this though, that you will start living it, so expect it. You will experience seasons of victory and rest and seasons of dealings.

So where are you at right now? If your spiritual muscles are straining and you feel that the Lord is cutting you down to bare essentials, then rejoice!

> *"John 15:2 Every branch in Me that does not bear*
> *fruit He takes away; and every branch that bears*
> *fruit He prunes, that it may bear more fruit.*
> *3 You are already clean because of the word which I*
> *have spoken to you.*
> *4 Abide in Me, and I in you. As the branch cannot*
> *bear fruit of itself, unless it abides in the vine,*
> *neither can you, unless you abide in Me."*

If you feel that pruning, then rejoice because the Lord saw something of value in you. He saw you as a branch worth pruning.

Allow Him to remove the dead branches from your life so that you can be fruitful once again. Then the next time you gear yourself for the race that is ahead, the weights will be gone. That rucksack will be empty.

You will not only run the race with endurance, but you will fly.

# 'Point To Remember' Summary

 Ready for your summary?

## Chapter 01: Guidelines to Mentorship

- Humans are born to mentor

- Write this down: What is the goal of this relationship?

- Having "lived it" gives you courage to be bold

- A Godly mentor finds his strength on his face before the Father

## Chapter 02: Guidelines to Discipleship

- If you are not experiencing success, then who you are needs to change.

- I never promised that it would be fair!

- God knows your flesh. Pressures expose your flesh so that you can see it for yourself.

- Your teaching and training should come from the same source

- Following through with one mentor ensures quick progress

## Chapter 03: Mentorship – The Bottom Line

- A sign that you found the right mentor is that you found someone to follow through with you no matter what.

- To walk in power is not about getting "more" but about "letting go"

## Chapter 04: Mentorship - What to Expect

- Mentorship is a natural ability that is learned

- Be a good mentor to qualify as a spiritual parent

- Mentorship is specific. Only one thing at a time

- Mentorship is 100% give

## Chapter 05: Start Here

- Memorize these two words: "I understand!"

- Do not be fooled by flattery

- Give acceptance when it is undeserved

- Identify the need – acceptance or recognition?

- Impartation takes place naturally when hearts are open

## Chapter 06: Mentorship: Do's & Don'ts

- No one is born knowing how to be a disciple

- Pray when the Holy Spirit tells you to pray

- You will change as much as they will

## Chapter 07: Phase 1 – The Mentorship Structure

- Everyone needs structure for successful learning

- How will you know if someone is ready? When you ask them!

- Once mentorship relationship is established. Get them into teachings

- Assume nothing. Until you give instruction, your disciple will not know what to do

- Sometimes in ministry mentorship, you will need to break from regular teachings and minister to hurts

- Mentorship is a science. Stick to the facts

- Just because you motivate and teach people, does not mean you are their mentor. You are their pastor.

## Chapter 08: Phase 2 - Parables, Problems and Projects

- Always apply your counsel to their training.

- It is up to you to bring your disciple to conviction. No conviction no change.

- Add spiritual wisdom to the naturalistic mentorship abilities

## Chapter 10: Phase 3: Chiseling and Correction

- Mentoring means shaping through removing from and adding to your disciple

- You cannot avoid bringing pressure. It is vital to the process

- You are molding your disciple into God's image – not yours.

- Watch out for your "blind spots" when bringing discipline

- Impartation is easy if you remove the hindrances first

## Chapter 11: How to Chisel

- Chisel using the Word, not your own ideas

- Stand in faith to chisel under the anointing

- The point of a chisel is to get a reaction

- It is not what happens to you in Life – It is how you respond that defines you

## Chapter 12: Healing, Impartation & Breaking Ties

- The point of this journey is to receive a gift at the end

- Identify sin by addressing how they responded to life – not what life did to them

- A good mentor guards the sheep and takes responsibility for their lives

- Never forget – demons gain license through sin

## Chapter 13: The Healing Process

- Without ministering healing, your job is incomplete

- Once you have studied all the principles. forget about them and let the Spirit give you wisdom

- Hands-on training seals impartation

- Impartation is the capstone of your mentorship relationship

## Chapter 14: Breaking the Mentorship Ties

- Not all disciples "make it." Some hit a plateau

- Your job is done when your disciple matches you

- Spiritual parenting can only commence once mentorship is over

- The prize of mentorship is to see your disciple outshine you

# Recommendations by the Author

If you enjoyed this book, we know you will love the following titles.

## Called to the Ministry

By Colette Toach

God has put a purpose for your existence inside you. There is a driving force within you to accomplish something much greater than yourself and to fulfill the call of God on your life. However... how do you know what that calling is?

Colette Toach takes you by the hand and helps you to realize the call of God that has been whispering to you all along.

## How to Get People to Follow You

By Colette Toach

Just like Gideon, David, Peter and Moses who weren't born leaders, but were forged into leaders - so you can have the kind of crowd that will follow you anywhere. There is a strong leader inside of you yet. One who is admired, loved and sought out! Learn how to get people to follow you and fulfill the vision that God has given you.

Sharing from her own failures and triumphs, Colette hands you the keys to your success as a leader.

## The Minister's Handbook

By Colette Toach

This is your manual on effective ministry. Whether you are dealing with an unexpected demon manifestation or you need to give marital counsel, you will find the answers here.

Colette Toach gives it to you in plain language. She gives you the steps 1, 2, 3 of how to do what God has called you to do. Keep a copy on hand, because you will come back to it time and time again!

## Strategies of War

By Colette Toach

Warfare is a very important part of our Christian lives. Whether we know it or not, the enemy is always looking for a way to take down the children of God. Now it is time that you learned how to stop taking the hits and take the fight to him instead.

No more allowing the enemy to have his way. Take back your land and remove him from your life for good.

Your victory is at hand. So, take hold and allow Colette Toach to guide and teach you the strategy to tearing down the kingdom of darkness.

# Contact Information

To check out our wide selection of materials, got to:
www.ami-bookshop.com

Do you have any questions about any products?

**Contact us at**: +1 (760) 466 - 7679
(8am to 5pm California Time, Weekdays Only)

**E-mail Address**: admin@ami-bookshop.com

**Postal Address:**

> A.M.I
> 5663 Balboa Ave #416
> San Diego, CA 92111, USA

**Facebook Page:**
http://www.facebook.com/ApostolicMovementInternational

**YouTube Page:**
https://www.youtube.com/c/ApostolicMovementInternational

**Twitter Page:** https://twitter.com/apmoveint

**AMI Bookshop** – It's not Just Knowledge, It's **Living Knowledge**

## About the Author

Born in Bulawayo, Zimbabwe and raised in South Africa, Colette had a zeal to serve the Lord from a young age. Coming from a long line of Christian leaders and having grown up as a pastor's kid she is no stranger to the realities of ministry. Despite having to endure many hardships such as her parent's divorce, rejection, and poverty, she continues to follow after the Lord passionately. Overcoming these obstacles early in her life has built a foundation of compassion and desire to help others gain victory in their lives.

Since then, the Lord has led Colette, with her husband Craig Toach, to establish *Apostolic Movement International,* a ministry to train and minister to Christian leaders all over the world, where they share all the wisdom that the Lord has given them through each and every time they chose to walk through the refining fire in their personal lives, as well as in ministry.

In addition, Colette is a fantastic cook, an amazing mom to not only her 4 natural children, but to her numerous spiritual children all over the world. Colette is also a renowned author, mentor, trainer and a woman that has great taste in shoes! The scripture to "be all things to all men" definitely applies here, and the Lord keeps adding to that list of things each and every day.

How does she do it all? Page through every book and teaching to experience the life of an apostle firsthand and get the insight into how the call of God can make every aspect of your life an incredible adventure.

Read more at www.colette-toach.com

Connect with Colette Toach on Facebook!
www.facebook.com/ColetteToach

Made in the USA
Middletown, DE
05 February 2024

49160672R00169